Tales from the Desert

an Arabian Memoir

Stuart Crocker

To my wife and daughter
for their support and who also
shared some of these experiences.

Contents

Introduction

The aim of this book is not to provide a detailed, learned history of Arabia, nor indeed to provide an exhaustive analysis of the politics, religion and culture which prevail in that part of the world.

Although these are described in some detail and are referenced throughout, it is essentially the story of a British expatriate who journeyed to Saudi Arabia in 1979 as a young man to seek his fortune and to experience a foreign culture. I had imagined that this adventure would last for only a couple of years, but as things turned out, it lasted substantially longer.

Some of the experiences related in the following pages were amusing, many frustrating, some mystifying, while others were downright terrifying. It is my hope that through the telling of these stories which occurred in this strange, yet always fascinating land, the reader will gain an insight to a place which for many, remains largely unknown and impenetrable.

Chapter 1

Arrival - 1979

As I went down the aircraft steps, the darkness illuminated by the airport floodlights, I thought for a moment that I must be standing directly in the exhaust of one of the whistling turbofan engines of the British Airways Boeing 747 which had touched down ten minutes earlier.

It was eight in the evening on the 2nd July, 1979 and, as I would soon realise, the oppressive heat had nothing to do with the aircraft engines, the natural air temperature even at this hour, was a brisk forty degrees centigrade. How impossibly hot, I wondered, would it be at midday.

I had just landed at Dhahran Airport in the Eastern Province of Saudi Arabia, just a few miles away from the headquarters of my new employer, the Arabian American Oil Company (Aramco), the company which produced and refined all the oil within the Kingdom of Saudi Arabia. It was the largest oil producing company in the world and the one for whom I would now be working.

My long journey to reach there had not just begun at Heathrow, it had started some six months earlier when I had responded to an advertisement in one of the national Sunday papers offering eye-watering - to me at least - salaries for professionals who wished to work for the Arabian American Oil Company in Saudi Arabia.

I had sent off an application, enclosing my not very long curriculum vitae and had waited, without any great expectation, for a response. The response however did come and it came within two weeks. I was invited down to London for an interview and a medical at the very grand Grosvenor House on Park Lane. They clearly meant business.

I arrived at the hotel one frosty January morning and walked up the steps where the door was opened by a liveried doorman. At the reception desk I was directed to the sixth floor where the company had rented most of the suites and in which they were conducting interviews for the many different disciplines they needed to recruit.

Suites had also been set aside for a group of doctors and other staff to perform the medicals. Two things were evident, one that this company was in a hurry and two, it was clearly a company which had a lot of money and knew how to spend it!

I thought my interview went reasonably well and I was subsequently given a fairly routine medical examination by a Harley Street doctor. I was told by my interviewer a decision would be made quickly and I would be informed within the next two weeks.

True to their word, I received a phone call the following week offering me a position and advising that a written offer was in the post. Goodness me! It was one thing to idly dream about disappearing abroad on a new and exciting adventure, quite another to actually make the decision.

I immediately called my ever-supportive wife whose initial reaction was to say; 'Great, when do we leave?'

I explained to her that the job offer was conditional upon me being hired on a bachelor status contract. This meant that if I accepted, I would be going alone. Up until that point it had all been hypothetical, we had often discussed the possibility of working abroad, but had assumed that if and when an opportunity came along, we would both be going. Now would be a good time for a serious chat.

After a great deal of soul-searching over the next few days, we concluded that even though it meant we would be apart for the first time in our short married life, this was too good an opportunity to turn down.

We reasoned that it would only be for a relatively short period of time - two years at the most and that during that time, I would be able to return home on leave every four months and it would allow us in two short years to pay off our mortgage and 'to get ahead of the game' as it were. So when I received the written offer, I sent my acceptance by return.

And so it was that five months later, I found myself walking down those aircraft steps into the oppressive heat of an Arabian, July evening.

I was probably little different from the majority of my fellow passengers on that flight. I had been offered a well-paid job and, even more attractively, without the inconvenience of paying any bothersome income tax. Like many other expatriates, I planned to merely interrupt my UK career for two years to achieve a financial goal before returning home. My sojourn in the desert was therefore to be a strictly short term affair, or at least, so I thought at the time.

I had left London in 1979, but the use of the *Hijrah* calendar throughout much of Arabia meant that when I landed it was in fact only the year 1399 and I was shortly about to find out why. The line of almost four hundred disembarking passengers snaked its way across the tarmac and into the arrival hall where I was about to have my first shock.

It was utter chaos. There were long queues at each of the three open passport control booths and none of them appeared to be moving. I must have waited in my particular queue for the best part of an hour before I at last handed my passport to the officer. By the time it had been stamped and I was allowed to pass through to the barrier and into the baggage reclaim hall, virtually all the cases had been taken off the carousel and randomly thrown into a vast pile almost ten feet high.

Passengers scrambled to locate their cases which could have been anywhere in the mound. Once retrieved, every piece of luggage was subjected, without exception, to a thorough search conducted by a khaki uniformed customs officer. The technique was either to simply rummage roughly through the contents, or more frequently, just to turn the opened case upside down, spilling the entire contents across the inspection counter.

Having passed this 'inspection', the unfortunate owner then had to struggle to put everything back in his case, while being exhorted to hurry up by the customs officer, so the next suitcase could be examined in a similar fashion.

I had been well briefed during my pre-travel orientation in London about what was and was not permissible to bring into the Kingdom of Saudi Arabia. It was a long list.

Items which might insult Islamic sensibilities such as alcohol, pork and of course pornography were strictly prohibited. I was later to discover that the term 'pornography' in Saudi Arabia included any representation of the female and sometimes the male form, in which the entire body was not completely covered by loose fitting clothing. Any newspapers, books or magazines were therefore eyed suspiciously and often just tossed onto the confiscated pile without being checked. I will relate the story of the 'felt tip editors' later on.

I eventually emerged outside the arrival building into a maelstrom of shouts, waving arms and a bewildering array of message boards. At last I saw my name being held up on a small board by a ginger haired, bearded man who introduced himself to me as Andy and took my suitcase to his waiting car. We drove away from the melee outside the airport terminal and about fifteen minutes later passed through a couple of security checkpoints before arriving at the main gate of Dhahran. On the way, he informed me we would be working together. Andy showed the grey-uniformed guard his identity card and then wrote my name on a log sheet as a 'visitor'. We drove into the camp and ten minutes later arrived at his house which was a single storey affair. We went inside and he offered me a glass of orange juice while pouring himself a glass of clear liquid which I assumed to be lemonade. We chatted for a while and he outlined a few of the things which would take place over the next few days.

I had been advised during the interview and orientation programme that Aramco had its own compound - indeed that it was a small town, where all western employees were housed in a variety of accommodation types ranging from large single-storey bungalows standing in extensive manicured gardens, to more modern town houses. There were shops, restaurants, schools and even a cinema in addition to a multitude of sports facilities. These included swimming pools, tennis, racquetball and squash courts, athletics tracks, baseball pitches and even a bowling alley. It sounded great, the only problem was that for the moment, it was not for me.

The reason was that it was full. The company had hired so many new employees during the past twelve months that it had simply run out of space and were frantically expanding the camp to accommodate the influx. This expansion however had not yet been completed and for the time being, newly arrived employees like myself were being housed in a nearby temporary residential facility called a construction camp.

Dhahran North Construction Camp was the full title of the complex which would be my temporary home. It housed about five thousand men and was located a couple of miles north of the main company facility in Dhahran. The camp consisted of long white buildings called dormitories, which stood on steel girders some four feet above the sand. Each of the buildings was in a modular form thus allowing them to be dismantled, transported and re-erected at a different site. Depending upon the configuration of the dormitories and how many men were assigned to each room, the buildings could accommodate either 24, 36, 72, or 164 men. I had been temporarily assigned a single room in a 36 man dormitory and it was at this facility that Andy dropped me off later that evening.

After a fitful sleep during which I was ever conscious of the noisy air conditioner, I awoke the next morning at six thirty. My dormitory had shower facilities and toilets located centrally within the building. As I was brushing my teeth at the row of sinks, the man next to me, a Scotsman who had also arrived the previous evening, looked up and surveyed the scene through a small window. 'My God!' he announced in a broad Glasgow accent; 'We've landed on the fuckin' moon.'

Sure enough, I also looked out of the window. It was my first sight of the desert in daylight and have to confess the undulating sand disappearing into the distance in the harsh sunlight did indeed resemble the surface of the moon. Apart from a few rocks and what appeared to be the odd clump of dead vegetation, the scene was utterly desolate.

What the hell had I done?

Chapter 2

Orientation

If someone had worked in remote parts of the world, or been in military service, then living in a construction camp would possibly not seem a great deal different from environments experienced before. For me however, it was like nothing I had ever seen.

The uniform rows of identical units stretching away over the sand had something of the appearance of an army barracks, each numbered unit providing different standards of accommodation for the different ranks of employees. The camp housed over five thousand men of many different nationalities. For the most part, they formed the contractor workforce rather than those like me, who were direct employees of the company.

The total workforce of Aramco was a whopping fifty thousand which was augmented at that time by a contractor workforce of a further thirty thousand employed by a multitude of major construction companies. In those days these were mainly American companies such as Fluor Corporation, Parsons and Santa Fe.

The camp was functional, well run and spotlessly clean. There were separate dining halls for employees dependent upon their grade code and nationality. The type of cuisine on offer in the various dining halls catered for a variety of international tastes. There were numerous recreation rooms containing pool tables, table football and pinball machines all of which were similarly segregated by grade code.

Food was good and plentiful. You could eat multiple hearty meals every day and judging by the appearance of some of the residents, that's exactly what they did. A number of outdoor cinemas, as well as floodlit football and softball pitches completed the recreational activities available. The only problem was that it was typically forty-five degrees Celsius in the shade during the summer days, so outdoor activities were strictly nocturnal, hence the floodlights.

Just a word about 'softball'. This was not some kind of sexually transmitted disease as I had initially supposed it to be, but a less dangerous version of baseball played with a softer ball that did not require players to wear helmets, or other protection.

The company grade code structure also had different payrolls for different nationalities. This potentially made for situations where two individuals performing the same role on exactly the same grade code, might be paid vastly different salaries dependent solely upon their passport. At the top of the pyramid as one might imagine from the name Arabian *American* Oil Company, were American employees followed closely by Saudi nationals. UK and Western European employees came next, then other nationalities who were employed on what was called the Asian and Other Arab (AOA) payroll. These included various Arab nationals from a host of countries right across the middle east, such as Lebanon, Jordan and Egypt as well as employees from countries in the Indian sub-continent and the Far East, chiefly the Philippines.

A company as large and as multinational as Aramco was inevitably run with a fairly rigorous level of bureaucracy and my first initiation to this would be the 'New Hire Orientation'. The orientation would last two full days and cover everything you might need to know about the company and the country in which it operated. I had already attended an orientation in London prior to my departure, but this one was far more detailed.

Firstly there was the assignment of an all-important employee number - a number which would be committed to memory for the rest of my life, a mail box number - also memorised for life, my department name and code number together with organisation code. Then followed registration with the company medical facilities, industrial security and the housing office.

Identity photographs and fingerprinting completed the process before you were finally issued with your ID card, something which would be required to be shown frequently and which if lost, would create untold difficulties as well as incurring a company fine. The identity card was the size of a credit card and contained not only your photograph, but also your blood type, department and organisation codes as well as various coded security clearances.

The greatest difference between employment in Saudi Arabia and the UK, or indeed most parts of the world, is the fact that the employer, or sponsor was totally responsible for housing, feeding and providing medical care to its employees as well as paying the employee's salary. There was barely any aspect of the employee's existence for which the company would not have a department, or an individual to assist. Some might say the employee's life was completely controlled, but for someone newly arrived in a very alien land and separated from friends and family, this was not necessarily a bad thing.

Only later when one became more settled, might this seem to involve an element of control, but at the end of the day, we were all there voluntarily and being paid extremely well, so in my opinion it was all good.

Another difference between working in the UK at that time and working in Saudi Arabia was the interface with multiple nationalities which, though I always found interesting, it was sometimes undeniably frustrating. All employees of the company, even Saudi Arabs, were required to speak English which was the official company language except in its dealings with the Saudi government when Arabic was used exclusively.

So far so good, but problems inevitably arose in the potential misunderstandings of certain English expressions. Even our American cousins had different terms for many things and in those first few weeks one lesson I quickly learned was the difference in meaning between a rubber and an eraser when I innocently asked an American female secretary if she happened to have one!

In those days prior to satellite television and the other electronic methods of communication which we take for granted today, the company had its own television station which typically showed old American films and television programmes all suitably edited so as not to offend Muslim sensibilities. There could be no kissing, or indeed any displays of affection and certainly nothing which could remotely be considered as female nudity. In the unlikely event that there were any scenes in these otherwise innocuous films and programmes, the editing process consisted of completely removing any offending scenes along with the associated dialogue so that following the storyline was extremely difficult, if not downright impossible.

'Channel 55' as the company television station was called, also paused its programme transmissions during prayer times, two of which occurred during late afternoon and early evening. An image of the Dhahran mosque would be displayed with no audio accompaniment during these intervals which, depending upon the particular prayer, could be up to thirty minutes. I still have an image of this mosque etched upon my mind.

Aramco came into existence some years before there was a fully functioning Saudi government and had therefore developed its own extensive laws and procedures which, by the time I arrived, ran in tandem to those which had later been created by the government. Indeed many laws subsequently enacted by the government were lifted straight from various company manuals.

One such instance was driving. British and American employees were not required to take a driving test when applying for a Saudi driving licence as it was deemed that driving standards in those countries were sufficiently high. In order to drive company vehicles however, all employees were required to undertake a 'defensive driving' course and afterwards take a test.

The reason for this somewhat unusual terminology would become all too clear upon venturing on to public roads outside of the company complexes. Many expatriates have used the word 'crazy' to describe local driving conditions, but I would soon discover that this term didn't even begin to cover it. A level of impatience coupled with a fatalistic approach to life and a blatant disregard for personal safety, combined to make driving in Saudi Arabia a profoundly dangerous undertaking.

I duly showed up for the defensive driving course later that week along with about ten other new employees. The course was to last a whole day and comprised a classroom session followed the practical test. It was run naturally, by a Saudi and it began with the basics, the first question being; 'What is the first thing you must do before starting the engine and driving off?' The obvious answers such as 'fasten seat belts'.... 'adjust mirrors'.... 'adjust seat' etc. were all declared by the instructor to be wrong. The correct answer of course was to check beneath the vehicle to ensure that a local resident was not sleeping underneath while seeking shade from the fierce desert sun. How could I have missed that one?

Over that little hiccup, I duly went on to pass the Aramco Defensive driving test, which came of course with a certificate. A couple of weeks later I was issued with my Saudi drivers licence and I was henceforth permitted to drive company vehicles, or indeed any private vehicle on the wide open roads of Saudi Arabia.

As mentioned before, the standard of driving was truly appalling. In the short time I had been there, I had never previously witnessed such a never-ending spectacle of reckless driving. It wasn't too many months after I arrived, that the government announced its concern that deaths in the kingdom due to motor vehicle collisions had now begun to exceed the national birth rate. Considering that Saudis typically had very large families, often well in excess of half a dozen children and frequently into double figures, this took a considerable effort.

Chapter 3

The Company

At this point, I should say a few more words about my new employer, the Arabian American Oil Company.

Its history began with the initial prospecting for oil in the Arabian Peninsula in the late 1930s, following the earlier discovery of oil on the neighbouring island of Bahrain in 1932. The rights to carry out surveys on the mainland were granted by the first Saudi monarch, King Abdulaziz to Standard Oil of California.

After a number of disappointing dry wells were drilled, commercial quantities of oil were finally discovered at Well No. 7 in the area, which was geologically known as the Dammam Dome - a low, rocky hill some five miles south of what was then the small fishing village of Dammam on the Gulf coast.

The location of this well would later lead to the establishment of the adjacent site of Dhahran, the oil town and company headquarters to this day. Well No. 7 amazingly continued to produce oil well into the 1990s although the Dammam field was quite a small oilfield compared to the much larger ones which would be discovered in later decades. These would include the giant Ghawar field in the southern part of the Eastern Province and the equally vast, though more difficult to exploit, offshore Safaniyah field in the shallow waters of the northern Gulf. These are respectively the largest onshore and offshore oilfields found anywhere in the world and would be the foundation of Saudi Arabia's enormous oil wealth.

Back in 1937 however, once commercial quantities of oil had been proven, Standard Oil had been joined by Exxon, Mobil and Texaco to conduct further and more widespread exploration and to develop the infrastructure required to extract the oil and then pipe it to a newly built export refinery and tanker terminal at Ras Tanura, some fifty miles north of Dhahran.

By the time of my arrival in 1979, Aramco had become a mature company with production and refinery facilities in multiple locations throughout the Eastern Province as well as some more recent ones over on the Red Sea coast. The reason for the rapid expansion of the company's workforce at this time and part of the reason I had been recruited, was the huge increase in activity involved in developing what was called the Master Gas System.

For decades, ever since oil production had first begun, the associated gas which is invariably recovered with the oil, had been flared off. Anyone flying over the Arabian deserts at night could not have failed to notice hundreds of flames punctuating the darkness as far as the eye could see. These were the GOSPs (Gas Oil Separator Plants) from which the liquid oil would be separated and piped to the processing plants for refining and export while the associated gas was simply flared off.

The Master Gas System would end this wastefulness and capture the gas which would provide the feedstock for the plants manufacturing bi-products which were being established by the Royal Commission in two locations, one at Jubail in the Eastern Province and one at Yanbu on the Red Sea in the Western Province.

These industries were largely privately owned, but fell under the umbrella of the Saudi Basic Industries Corporation (SABIC). They would produce commodities such as fertilisers, polymers, ethylene, polypropylene and urea from the natural gas which had hitherto been wasted. The days of Saudi Arabia merely being an exporter of crude oil were rapidly coming to an end. The new diversified Saudi economy would henceforth produce items which had once been the province of industries in the more economically developed oil importing nations of the world.

With oil prices trading at an all-time high after the oil shock of 1973, money was rolling into the country at an unprecedented rate and the time was ripe to diversify and invest in downstream industries. Armies of construction workers, chiefly from South Korea, toiled relentlessly to build new industrial cities from scratch. Roads, port facilities, drainage canals, housing, schools and shops, everything in fact required to support these mammoth projects and all rising up from hitherto barren patches of sand along the coast.

Hyundai, the South Korean company better known these days as a car manufacturer, was one of the biggest construction contractors. Their thousands of employees, identically dressed in grey overalls, would travel from accommodation camps to the building sites every morning in fleets of yellow buses. Their resemblance to an army was not far short of the mark as indeed, the majority of these employees had elected, with their government's permission, to sign up with Hyundai and work in Saudi Arabia as an alternative and more lucrative option, to performing the two years of national service which would otherwise have been required had they stayed in their homeland.

Along with my other personal effects, I had arrived in this country armed with T.E. Lawrence's *Seven Pillars of Wisdom*. The land in which I now found myself however, bore only a superficial resemblance to that described by Lawrence of Arabia when fighting in the desert some sixty years earlier. The rapid rise in oil revenues was transforming not only the landscape of the country, but its culture along with it.

From the not so far-off days when King Abdulaziz, the founding monarch, travelled around his kingdom with the entire contents of the national treasury in chests, strapped to the backs of a few camels, the country had become rich beyond its wildest dreams. The enormous reservoirs of oil which lay beneath the endless miles of sand were being pumped to the surface and sold hour after hour, minute by minute for up to a hundred dollars per barrel. By 1979, they could pump seven million of those barrels each and every day and as far as the Saudis were concerned, it was a God-given gift.

Chapter 4

Getting Down to Work

Dhahran North Office Complex was a collection of twenty large, temporary office buildings located about half a mile from the residential camp. They certainly weren't as swish as the more glamorous steel and glass offices on the main camp complex, but at least I didn't have far to commute.

The office buildings were large, square portables standing on steel girder frames some four feet off the ground. They were built from separate sections and could typically accommodate around eighty people. Each building was assigned a number and mine was No. 17. My office was situated along one of the outer walls and had a small window and a door out onto a corridor which ran around the building. On the inside of the corridor in the centre of the building were the open plan, or 'bullpen' areas as they were called by the Americans, which were occupied by lower grade employees and contractors.

My immediate work colleagues were of various nationalities, most of the senior positions were filled by Americans and Canadians while those lower down the scale were filled by Indians, Pakistanis and Filipinos. We 'Brits' as the Americans usually referred to us, were a comparatively recent innovation within the company and this had necessitated the creation of an entirely new UK/Western European payroll. This provided for salaries and employee benefits which were somewhat different to the salaries and benefits enjoyed by our north American cousins.

I was nevertheless happy to be there and had no particular concerns that my salary might be exceeded by that of others, as no doubt my salary and benefits exceeded others below me in the company hierarchy. As far as I was concerned, I was on a good package and as I only intended to remain for a year or two, I wasn't unduly concerned.

The company had a large number of Saudi Arab employees making up around half of the workforce. In my department they were invariably younger than me and occupied lower level positions. It was written into the job descriptions of all expatriates that one of your duties was to train Saudi nationals to ultimately take over your position. These young men were the future of the company and it was only appropriate that in due course the requirement for western expertise would decline as educational standards within Saudi Arabia improved.

Although Saudis were without exception Muslims, I discovered that there were different types of Muslims. Before travelling to Saudi Arabia, I had assumed that all Muslims were the same, but it soon became apparent even among the Aramco workforce, that there was a distinction between those who followed the orthodox Sunni version of Islam and those of the Shia persuasion.

To a non-Muslim these differences were imperceptible, but differences there certainly were. They prayed in slightly different ways and the Shia observed some festivals which the Sunni did not. The differences could possibly be equated to the Catholic

- Protestant split in Christianity, although the Islamic schism was for entirely different historical and theological reasons.

While forming only a small minority of the overall Saudi population - less than ten percent, the Shia almost exclusively resided in the Eastern Province, particularly round the oasis town of Qatif and its surrounding villages. Qatif was only twenty miles away from Dhahran and consequently the proportion of Shia employees in Aramco was something like fifty percent, far higher than the national proportion.

Generally they were hard working individuals, but it was noticeable that while many of the lower grade positions in the company were held by Shia, or 'Qatifis' as we called them, the senior management positions were drawn mainly from the Sunni community. Although there was no overt sectarianism, it seemed that a glass ceiling was firmly in place.

Working with these young Saudis, whom I found to be unfailingly polite and friendly, I rapidly became aware of a term widely used in the Arab world – *Insh'allah*. This literally means 'If God wills it' and is used frequently during everyday conversations, particularly the end of a sentence when something is planned to happen at some point in the future. Expressions such as 'see you tomorrow' would inevitably end with the words *Insh'allah*. It was a sign of their fatalistic nature, but it was also used as something of an excuse should things not go to plan, or appointments be missed.

The nature of the business in which I was involved was the supply of short-term contractor manpower to supplement the many gaps in the company's own workforce at this time of unprecedented expansion. Sixteen firms of varying sizes provided this expertise, with men recruited primarily from the United States, United Kingdom, India and the Philippines. The Resident Managers of each company, together with a small support staff were all housed in the same building for ease of communication.

Each of these firms had the opportunity to fill each and every supplementary manpower requisition which was transmitted to us from the various departments throughout Aramco, which were called 'Users'. The salary levels and employment packages were identical between the companies for each grade code and nationality, so they competed with one another purely on the basis of being able to provide the best qualified candidates. The companies would then be paid a profit and overhead percentage on top of the man's salary and benefits - typically in the range of ten to fifteen percent although these percentages varied slightly between contractors.

In true Aramco fashion, the terms and conditions of these contractor employees mirrored those of their own employees with a few significant changes - the working hours were forty eight hours based on a six day week rather than the forty hours based on a five day week which applied to its own employees. Salaries were typically fifteen percent lower than Aramco employee salary scales with no additional benefits other than standard vacation entitlements.

Accommodation would always be in a construction camp and the twelve month contracts were renewable with joint agreement. Items such as sick leave payment, salary increases upon contract renewal, terminations, or any other matter were determined by Aramco and not by the individual's actual employer. When I arrived, there were approximately 1,500 contractor employees working under this scheme and integrated into the regular Aramco workforce, but within two years this had expanded to 2,500.

In many ways, the working environment was not so different to that at home, but every now and again I was forcefully reminded just which part of the world I was in. One such occasion happened after I had been there just a couple of weeks. On an otherwise quiet, hot afternoon, there came a knock on my office door and a diminutive Saudi policeman, clad in khaki put his head around. He clearly spoke little or no English, but gestured politely to me that he might be allowed to come in.

I immediately got up from my chair and ushered him in, but noticed as he entered my office, that one of his wrists was handcuffed to someone else. The other handcuff was attached to the wrist of a westerner who followed him into the room. He was further handcuffed to yet another policeman and the three of them shuffled into my small office. Shuffle was the appropriate word as I saw to my horror that in addition to the handcuffs, the westerner was also shackled around his ankles.

The three of them eventually manoeuvred themselves towards the seats and I gestured for them to sit down. As the policemen spoke no words of English, it was left to their prisoner who turned out to be an American, to explain exactly how he came to be in this situation. In the meantime and ever conscious of Arab hospitality, I called for the tea-boy and had him bring cups of tea for them. It was certainly entertaining to watch three men trying to drink tea while handcuffed together.

The American explained that he had been stopped while driving and the police had found alcohol in his car. This of course was a serious offence and they had promptly arrested him and taken him to the police station. All expatriates in

Saudi Arabia had a sponsor who was usually their employer and who was responsible for the actions of their employees. His employer was one of the contractor companies which was managed by my department and this was why he had been brought to this particular building.

Once I understood the situation, I contacted his resident manager whose office was in the same building and he came along with his government affairs man who was, as always, a Saudi. The government affairs man spoke at length with the police in Arabic and eventually the group left my office. It turned out that the American had been supplying large quantities of alcohol. Unfortunately for him, he had been stopped for some minor traffic offence upon which they discovered the alcohol contained in plastic jerrycans in the boot of his car.

I'm not sure what happened to him. He may have received a lengthy prison sentence, or might even have been flogged. More likely he would have been quietly deported. Much depended upon the nationality of the offender, the influence of the various government affairs men and more crucially the attitude of the local police commander. On the one hand they might wish to make an example of anyone caught, 'pour encourager les autres', yet on the other hand they didn't necessarily want their jails full of westerners with all the attendant international publicity that such incarceration might bring.

Saudi prisons had a well-earned reputation for harsh conditions and were definitely not a place you wanted to find yourself. The conditions were basic to say the least… medieval in fact. Multiple prisoners were kept in large cells and they typically slept on the floor. Toilet facilities consisted of a metal pail in the corner of the cell and as for washing… well, you didn't. More importantly, the prisoners were not provided with food by the prison authorities, so meals had to be brought to them by either family members, or in the case of foreigners by their employers.

Fortunately, I only ever entered a Saudi prison as a visitor, although I did spend a few nervous hours in some other Middle Eastern jails some years after, but more of that later.

Chapter 5

The Joys of Ramadan

The holy month of Ramadan commenced just a few weeks after my arrival in Saudi Arabia. I was aware that it was the Muslim month of fasting, but I had no idea just how seriously this was taken by the locals. Far from being a religious observance purely for the Muslims, everyone, regardless of faith, had to observe the fast which lasted from sunrise until sunset, at least in public.

Nothing had quite prepared me for this. At work, office doors which had hitherto remained open were now firmly shut and sometimes locked. The reason for this was that none of us could be seen to be drinking tea, coffee, or water in public during daylight hours. We non-Muslims scurried around hiding our cups and glasses before secretively drinking the contents behind closed office doors. I felt like a naughty schoolboy.

Inevitably the Muslims in the workplace knew what was going on, but in all the years I was there, never once did I hear a word of complaint about this behaviour. It was a case of recognising that Muslims were fasting which was an undeniable hardship, especially when the fasting month fell in the heat of summer. Care was therefore taken not to overtly offend anyone's sensibilities by drinking, or eating openly, in the knowledge that they could not. Naturally, all restaurants, cafes and other eating establishments were closed during daylight hours for the entire month.

Due to the *Hijrah* or lunar calendar, Ramadan occurred at different times of the year, basically twelve days earlier each year when measured against the Gregorian calendar. In my first year in Saudi Arabia, Ramadan fell in late July.

Lying close to the Tropic of Cancer, Saudi Arabian hours of daylight didn't vary greatly between midsummer and midwinter. For the religious, a white thread was traditionally held up to the sky at dusk and when it was no longer possible to discern the colour of the thread, the night was deemed to have begun and the fast could be broken, but only after performing prayers.

Residents of urban areas relied upon the firing of a cannon to announce that it was indeed time to end the daily fast and cannons were strategically positioned in many towns and villages for this purpose. This first meal at the end of the day was called *Iftar* and it was a time of joyous celebration... not to mention profound relief.

Working hours during this month of fasting were normally seven in the morning until four in the afternoon and generally remained so for non-Muslims, but for Muslims the hours were seven in the morning until midday. They therefore worked only five hours, but were still paid for eight. Typically, the Saudis and other Muslims would go home after work to sleep for the remainder of the afternoon then rise just before sundown. After prayers, they would drink, eat and party until late into the night and often into the early hours.

They effectively turned night into day, though they might grab a few hours' sleep before dragging themselves into work the following morning. Productivity, not high at the best of times, would plummet during the holy month and the company was basically run entirely by expatriates during this period.

The *Mutawain* were the religious police of Saudi Arabia, more properly known as The Committee for the Promotion of Virtue and the Prevention of Vice. They were usually elderly men with shorter robes, called *thobes* who carried camel canes and were often accompanied by a uniformed policeman. Always evident in the local towns of Al Khobar and Dammam, their duties were to keep a watchful eye on public places and to berate, sometimes with a stick, anyone they deemed either to be inappropriately dressed, or behaving without due decorum. They would also ensure that shopkeepers promptly shut their premises at prayer calls and encouraged the faithful to hasten to the nearest mosque.

They were particularly vigilant during Ramadan, ensuring the fast was rigorously observed by all. One expatriate, a chain smoker, related an incident to me about the time he had visited a bank in Al Khobar during the morning and upon leaving the premises, had lit up a cigarette, quite forgetting it was Ramadan. He was observed by a *mutawa* who quickly summoned a policeman.

The expatriate thought that such a breach might result in him being taken to the police station and was understandably nervous. He was told in broken English by the policeman that he should not smoke in public and would doubtless have escaped with just an admonishment. He was however so relieved to be dealt with in such a lenient manner, that he unthinkingly lit up another cigarette and was promptly arrested.

For expatriates working in Aramco, it was quite a pleasant

time with many things being delayed, or put on hold until the following month. In the afternoons when all the Muslims had finished work for the day, things were generally very quiet and relaxed and people could drink and eat openly without having to hide behind closed office doors.

The end of Ramadan signalled the commencement of the five day Feast of *Eid al-Fitr*, or 'Feast of Ending the Fast' This was ostensibly the Muslim version of Christmas, a time of joy when gifts were exchanged and lavish parties thrown to celebrate the end of the holy month. It was also a national holiday and many expatriates, if they hadn't already departed earlier in the month, would fly out to take advantage of the holiday which normally lasted for five days.

Chapter 6

Moving into Town

I lived on the construction camp for three months before space was eventually found for me on the main camp. I was advised I would initially be moving into temporary housing until a more permanent residence became available.

Temporary housing for employees on bachelor status basically meant that it was shared - usually by three, or sometimes four people of the same sex. I visited the Housing Department to see exactly what was on offer and it transpired that there were two available houses, each of which had four bedrooms, two shared bathrooms with showers, a communal lounge and a shared kitchen.

They were generally older properties, which in some cases dated from the 1940s and 1950s and had at one time been family homes for an earlier generation of Aramco employees. I was given the addresses of two houses and a set of keys for each. The houses were in the older part of camp, barely a ten minute walk from the housing office. I duly looked over the two houses. They both had a similar layout, tiled floors and sparse company issued furniture.

The big difference between the two, was that while one was a nondescript affair constructed of what appeared to be lightweight asbestos-like panels, the other one looked like no other house I had seen anywhere on the camp. Constructed of stone with sand coloured stucco facing, it rose up like a miniature fortress with small towers at each corner, one of which even boasted a flagpole. I knew it had to be this one. An Englishman's home really would be his castle, albeit a temporary one.

I later discovered that the building's somewhat unusual appearance was due to the fact it had been built for use as a post office in the 1940s. The most important thing of course would be the people with whom I would be sharing this grand, though spartan abode which at the moment was completely empty. Upon my return to the housing office to sign the assignment forms, I asked if they knew who my fellow housemates were likely to be. I was merely told it would be three fellow British employees who, like me were currently housed off camp. So it was that I packed up the meagre belongings in my room and bade farewell to the construction camp.

I was on my own in the 'fort' for a few days before my new house mates moved in. It turned out we were all about the same age and had arrived in Saudi Arabia within days of each other. An instant bond was formed.

We all worked in different areas of the company. One was an industrial chemist, one an IT specialist and the other a buyer of foodstuffs for the company supermarket, or commissary as it was known. At least I wouldn't be on my own for the rapidly approaching Christmas Day and as a further bonus I soon became acquainted with the fact that alcohol was available on the main camp if you knew where to look. It also occurred to me that I would no longer have the daily luxury of prepared meals and would now have to buy food and cook for myself.

The Aramco commissary was a large supermarket much the same as you find at home, the products were largely imported from the United States, though there were also some familiar British brands. Part of the commissary at that time was accessed by a separate door. This was the 'Pork Store'.

The company had been given a dispensation by the Saudi government many years earlier to import and sell pork products in their own commissaries. The sale of these products was however strictly controlled and limited to non-Muslim senior staff. There was also a monthly limit to the amount which could be spent in the pork store in order to discourage re-selling on the black market.

One of the most common rumours which used to circulate among the expatriate community was that the pork store was about to shut. It traditionally closed each year during Ramadan for reasons which were never entirely clear to me, but the rumour was always that it wouldn't re-open. The rumour was an annual favourite, but inevitably during the late 1980s it at last became reality, the pork store closed its doors a final time and was consigned to the realms of history. A kind of self-fulfilling prophecy.

In those days December 25th was designated as a company holiday, though of course outside the Aramco camps there were no visible signs of it being Christmas. In Dhahran however, some residents really went overboard, completely covering their houses in coloured lights and placing extravagant illuminated displays of reindeer and sleighs on their front lawns. It seemed to be less about the celebrations and more about making a statement about the complete lack of any Christmas observations outside the fence and the all-pervading influence of Islam throughout our daily lives.

My particular festivities started early with drinks straight after work on Christmas Eve followed by a turkey dinner at a friend's house. At the end of the night, I foolishly accepted a lift home from one of the attendees who had a company pick-up truck. I knew it was a bad decision the moment he pulled away at high speed. We eventually made it onto the Golf Course Road, a dual carriageway which connected the older part of main camp with the more recently built Dhahran Hills, half a mile away.

The dual carriageway had a high central median punctuated with street lights and palm trees. It also had a long curve and it was clear that at the speed he was driving, he was not going to make it. Just after the entrance to the Golf Club House, he duly mounted and crossed the central median - not a difficult task for the four wheel drive Dodge truck.

Unfortunately there was a car coming in the opposite direction and despite my shouts to stop, the wild man decided to drive back over the central median, this time clipping a palm tree and demolishing a lamppost. The impact caused the truck to rollover three times before coming to rest upside down in the sand at the far side of the road. Seconds seemed like an eternity and although I was wearing a seat belt, I felt sure that I was going to die.

My first recollection was of hanging upside down in the upturned cab. The engine was still running and blood was everywhere. I managed to unbuckle the seat belt and reached across to turn off the engine, afraid that the truck would burst into flames at any moment. Thankfully it didn't.

The driver appeared dead, his head trapped between the crushed roof of the cab and the seat back, blood pouring from his head. To this day, I do not know how I extricated myself from the vehicle as the cab roof had been crushed flat with the bonnet of the truck. Aramco Industrial Security and an ambulance were on the scene within minutes and with the use of cutting equipment, managed to extricate the driver and take him off to the hospital. I was convinced that if he wasn't already dead, he shortly would be.

I was in something of a daze and stumbled around by the side of the road near the wrecked truck. Amazingly, I had no visible injuries except for the tiniest of cuts on my little finger. When asked by the security personnel whether I had seen anything, I decided to lie, saying only that I had been walking home and came upon the crash moments after it had happened. They clearly believed me as they thought that it would surely have been impossible for anyone to walk away from the wreck.

There was nothing else I could do, so still somewhat dazed and not a little drunk, I walked home. Destroying a company vehicle, particularly while under the influence of alcohol was a termination offence and although I had only been a passenger, I was wary of somehow being implicated in the incident. Judging by the state of the driver when he was pulled from the wreckage, I imagined getting fired was the least of his problems.

The following day I rang a mutual friend and told him what had happened. He agreed to go to the hospital and find out how the driver was. He had miraculously survived the crash with just a fractured skull and his injuries were not considered to be life threatening. The doctors said that when he regained consciousness he had been asking about his passenger. No-one thought it possible that anyone could have been in the vehicle and they put it down to post-traumatic ramblings.

I decided that I had nothing to hide and so went to the hospital to visit him the following day. The heavily bandaged man who had almost killed me was filled with contrition. He made a full recovery and was discharged from hospital some weeks later upon which his employment was terminated for the misuse of a company vehicle.

It was about this time that the Grand Mosque siege took place in Mecca. Politics and religion were never strangers in Saudi Arabia and although it was an autocracy run by the king and the rest of the Al Saud dynasty, the system was not to everyone's taste.

Ever since the rise of the Al Saud and the foundation of what became Saudi Arabia, the ruling family had aligned themselves closely with religious leaders. In particular, they followed the teachings of Abdullah Ibn Wahab an 18th century cleric who hailed from the same oasis town of Ad Diriyah as the Al Saud. Wahhabism as it came to be known, was merely a very austere and fundamental interpretation of the Qur'an.

Like all new recruits I had been advised on the history and religion of the country and that the centre of Islamic culture was the Grand Mosque in Mecca. Imagine my surprise when I learned that the holiest place in Islam, had not only been attacked by a group of rebels, but had in fact been taken over by them and was now under siege by the Saudi army. This had never happened before and the country was in a profound state of shock.

Little was known about the group and though it seemed that many were Saudis, what they wanted to achieve was unclear.

Mecca was off limits to non-Muslims, but as the siege went on there was an increasing clamour for the authorities to take firm action which they ultimately did. It was rumoured afterwards that the Saudis had enlisted the assistance of French special forces, who were very probably not Muslims. This however was never confirmed.

The surviving perpetrators were duly tried, convicted and beheaded in a number of cities around the kingdom as a warning to others. Since that event, the kings of Saudi Arabia have styled themselves as 'Custodians of the Two Holy Mosques' - Mecca and Medina.

It turned out that Saudi Arabia might not be quite the sleepy and peaceful backwater I had imagined.

Chapter 7

Dying For a Drink

If anyone had ventured out to Saudi Arabia to cure a drink problem, it was most assuredly a big mistake. The fact that it was illegal, somehow gave the consumption of alcohol a frisson of excitement and a sense of danger not present at home. Combined with the fact that homemade booze was both cheap and plentiful, many people consumed far greater quantities of alcohol in Saudi Arabia than they had hitherto done at home.

There were basically three types of homemade alcohol available, alcohol spirit called *Siddiqui* or *sid*, although the Americans customarily called it 'white'. *Siddiqui* is a colloquial Arabic term for friend, or mate, so it was an appropriate name. It was produced by a distillation process using the three simple ingredients of water, sugar and yeast.

In the years prior to my arrival, stills for making alcohol had actually been issued by the company to American expatriates upon their arrival, together with an operating manual entitled *The Blue Flame*. Even after this practice had been discontinued, all company houses, even new ones, were designed with 'still cupboards', windowless rooms usually leading off the garage. They always had the essential water and electricity supply.

The first stage of production involved a large plastic dustbin into which sugar, water and yeast were poured and then left to ferment for a few days. This mixture was called the 'mash'. There were many variations in the still equipment, some had been issued by the company and some had more recently been illicitly fabricated in the company's mechanical workshops.

Regardless of age and type, they all performed the same basic task of boiling the mash under pressure to distil the alcohol. This process was repeated three times to ensure purity and a basic absence of any real flavour. The final product was neat, or uncut alcohol. A gallon of uncut 'third run *sid*' commanded a price of 350 Saudi riyals, the equivalent of around one hundred and twenty dollars. 'Uncut' however, was not the way it was drunk. It was usually cut by the addition of an equal measure of pure water in order that the drink would not completely blow your head off!

The finished article would typically be taken with ice and either tonic, or coke and a slice of lemon. Surprisingly, it was quite a pleasant drink and not dissimilar to vodka, or gin. For those who preferred a darker drink more akin to whisky, oak chips were added to the final product and allowed to soak for a period of time. This process imbued the spirit with a golden colour and some thought, a more mellow flavour.

Within the company communities, water and electricity were provided free of charge so once you had either purchased, manufactured, or been given the still, the only expenses in producing this type of alcohol were the large quantities of sugar and small amounts of yeast. It always amused me that stores and supermarkets throughout Saudi Arabia sold sugar in large hessian sacks as though it were perfectly normal for people to have such a sweet tooth.

The cost of producing a gallon of uncut *Siddiqui* was around twenty Saudi riyals - about six dollars. The profit margin, should you elect to sell it, was therefore in the region of one thousand percent and it was hardly surprising that such a tempting margin prompted some expats to operate their stills on a semi-commercial basis. Indeed some, who shall we say, did not have the most demanding of jobs, or those who could legitimately be away from their usual place of work for extended periods of time, became almost full-time still operators and were in many cases able to earn more from this activity, than their already high salaries. The risk of course was not an economic one, but very much the case that this was an illegal activity and one could end up getting into serious hot water.

The individuals engaged in larger scale production were referred to as the 'booze barons' and although some were eventually caught and jailed, more often than not the company terminated their employment and quietly repatriated them. The major risk was being turned in by someone who held a personal grudge, but occasionally these activities came to the attention of the authorities because of an accident.

Accidents usually happened when the distiller was either away from the house, or at least not present in the still room during the run. The term 'baby-sitting' was used to describe the long and tedious chore of watching over the still during its operation and many operators would often leave the still running for periods of an hour or more without being present.

Everything was fine unless there was either a mechanical problem with the still itself, usually a leak, or when the water, or power supply was cut off. A power outage was merely an inconvenience, but a cut in the water supply could lead to a significant elevation in still temperatures. If it was not turned off promptly, the situation could become highly explosive. One operator discovered this to his cost when he returned home one day to find his garage doors had been completely blown off and the company's security personnel in attendance. Needless to say his employment in Saudi Arabia came to a premature end.

Aside from these incidents, many of the booze barons operated discreetly for years and became very wealthy in the process.

The second type of alcoholic drink was wine which was unsurprisingly made from grape juice. An Austrian brand called *Rausch,* or a concentrated grape juice sold under the brand name *Sodap* which was imported from Greece, were both available in the commissary and in local stores. The addition of yeast and sugar to these liquids when poured into a plastic barrel, would commence the fermentation process which could take a number of weeks, the exact time being dependent upon the ambient temperature.

After bottling, it required some time for the impurities to settle and then it had to be decanted before it could finally be drunk. I have to say, that no matter which recipe was used, I never found any of the wines to be particularly palatable, despite the ludicrous claims of some producers that it was almost as good as the 'real thing'.

The third type of alcohol available was beer. This was typically made from a product called *Vitabake* sold in cans with a label describing the contents as 'Malt Syrup for Baking'. This again was freely available, not only in the commissary, but in many stores in the local cities. Similar to sugar, it was purchased by expatriates in such industrial quantities that the locals must have thought that we ate an extraordinarily large number of cakes.

Making beer was a much simpler process, mixing the syrup together with the indispensable ingredients of water, sugar and yeast. Even better, it only took a couple of weeks to ferment the brew in a large plastic dustbin before bottling and then leaving it for another couple of weeks before drinking, or sometimes less if you were desperate.

In later years the importation of non-alcoholic beer simplified this process. Sold in tins, the beer was poured into a large vat and with the addition of sugar and yeast, hey presto, was re-fermented to produce an eminently palatable beverage.

The aforementioned *Rausch* bottles were not merely the containers for grape juice, they had a real value. With their ceramic corks and rubber seals, operated on a levered wire system, they provided a perfect airtight seal. They proved to be extremely effective and durable as beer bottles, as the pressure of the contents was maintained even after lengthy periods of storage. No residence was complete without at least a dozen cartons of *Rausch* bottles scattered somewhere about the place.

Despite the complete ban on alcohol within Saudi Arabia, it was actually possible to buy the real thing provided you knew the right people. For practical purposes, this black market existed only in spirits and more specifically Johnnie Walker whisky, which for some reason was the drink of choice for those Saudis who chose to ignore their religious precepts.

A bottle of this would cost 300 Saudi riyals - around a hundred dollars in those days. It was also possible to obtain a bottle of vodka, or gin at similar prices. Most expats however made their own alcohol, or at least they made their own beer and wine. If they did not possess a still of their own, they could easily purchase a gallon of *sid* from someone who did.

I had arrived in Arabia thinking that the production of oil was the paramount concern of the expatriate workforce, but I soon discovered that it was in fact the production of alcohol. I sometimes idly wondered whether the volume of alcohol produced in the various company residential camps might actually exceed the production of oil.

Chapter 8

Bahrain by Dhow

The company had a very active employees association called the Aramco Employees Association (AEA) which organised many activities and trips. Self-directed groups under the auspices of this organisation were given funding by the company and allowed the use of various company facilities. These groups were many and varied with activities ranging from traditional sports, to handicrafts, art and drama, even including the unlikely 'Arabian Hoedowners'.

There were organised trips to local places of interest within the Eastern Province such as Qatif and Hofuf. One such trip being organised not too long after my arrival caught my eye. This was a very reasonably priced dhow trip to the neighbouring island and country of Bahrain. Today it is linked by a fifteen mile long causeway which, back then was still in the early stages of construction. Bahrain at that time was only accessible by air or sea. It was said that the short ten minute flight from Dhahran was one of the most expensive international flights in the world weighing in at a hefty fifty dollars per mile.

The trip appealed to the romantic in me and I thought it might be something of an adventure. Travelling by dhow and spending the weekend in the more liberal environment of

Bahrain sounded like fun. A few friends and I, passports in hand complete with exit re-entry visas boarded the company bus which took us the short five-mile journey to the small dhow port at Al Khobar.

The trip proved popular and two dhows had been chartered for the journey which would take more than three hours in the ancient vessels equipped with equally ancient motors. The sea between Saudi Arabia and Bahrain is very shallow, averaging only twenty feet with just one or two deeper channels here and there. As the motors chugged away, the low-lying Bahraini coast eventually came into view. The captain swung the dhow on a more northerly course to take us in the direction of the capital, Manama.

Large hotels and office buildings were clustered around the port area and the noise of car horns and hum of traffic, indicated that this was indeed a bustling city. A bus awaited us at the quayside and we were given a tour of the island for a few hours. Bahrain is the only island state in the whole of Arabia and, measuring a mere fifteen miles by ten, it is the smallest of all the Gulf states. It therefore didn't take too long to see the highlights.

The tour included the old spice market in Manama, the Amiri palaces at Riffa in the centre of the island and Riffa Fort, an eighteenth century stronghold of the Al Khalifa ruling family. At that time, the small island nation was styled as the 'State of Bahrain' and was ruled over by the diminutive Sheikh Isa bin Salman Al Khalifa. This would later change after his death to the Kingdom of Bahrain ruled by his eldest son King Hamad, but more of that later.

Sheikh Isa had a summer palace down by the beach on the

south west coast of the island. Members of the public were allowed to use these beaches and this is where we were to spend the night. I slept on the sand with a case of beer for my pillow... it was certainly a cheap and cheerful expedition.

The highlight of the following day was a visit to one of the venerable older hotels in the heart of Manama, The Delmon Hotel - named after the ancient civilisation which once flourished on the island. The major attraction of course was the bar where we could be served proper drinks and all legally. This was our first proper drink for more than three months and to say that the ice-cold beers went down well is something of an understatement.

It was soon time to re-board the dhows, but the trip organiser had seen fit to load on board some cooled cases of beer for the journey back. The dhows chugged out of Manama port as we popped the ring pulls. Five cases of beer had been loaded into each dhow, but as ours was full of single young men as opposed to some families on the other one, the rate of consumption varied considerably. By the time we were half way across, our beer had all gone while on the other boat, sailing just fifty yards away, we could see that they had barely consumed two cases.

Despite our shouts for them to transfer at least one of their unused cases into our boat before we entered Saudi waters, our pleas went unanswered. We were only an hour or so away from the point at which any unopened beer would have to be thrown overboard. Clearly more radical tactics would have to be employed.

We had a word with the captain, who had been merrily swigging beer with the rest of us ever since leaving Bahrain.

He was very enthusiastic about the idea of 'boarding' the other dhow to take possession of their remaining beer. Piracy on the high seas was afoot.

The captains of the two vessels were shouting to each other in Arabic and laughing uproariously as we inched closer together. We of course were shouting 'prepare to board' and other lines we recalled from old pirate movies. Finally the trip organiser, travelling on the other boat and fearing the worst, reluctantly threw two cases of beer over to us as we came alongside. With a cheer from all on board we moved away amid a fizz of opening cans and a resumption of our drinking. With a bit of luck we would finish them before arrival.

We almost achieved this, but had to leave half a dozen unopened cans on a sand spit, a couple of miles from the Saudi shore. It was no great loss and we docked in Al Khobar knowing that we would not be drinking any more of the real stuff for quite a while.

Chapter 9

The King is Dead, Long Live the King

When I first arrived in Saudi Arabia, the monarch was King Khaled who had assumed the throne after the assassination of his elder brother, Faisal five years earlier. In the Al Saud family, the monarchy customarily passes from elder brother to the next eldest brother, rather than from father to son as in most other monarchical systems. Faisal and Khalid were the eldest sons of the nation's founder, King Abdulaziz who had sired an extraordinary number of children with his multiple wives and concubines during his lifetime.

In all, he is said to have fathered some forty five sons and a similar number of daughters. Little wonder that the pecking order within the royal family was labyrinthine to say the least. The first son to succeed King Abdulaziz when he died in 1953 had been Saud. Although the kingdom was newly rich with oil revenues, alas, he did not prove to be a wise king.

He fiercely argued with a number of his brothers before he was eventually deposed in 1964 and sent into exile. He was replaced by Faisal who proved to be a competent and wise ruler, remaining on the throne for eleven years until 1975 when he was killed by his nephew at an audience in the palace in Riyadh. The motives for the murder remain unclear, though the official line was that he died at the hands of a 'deranged nephew'.

Next up was Khalid, yet another brother and he was the man on the throne when I arrived. Already an elderly man with a long-standing heart condition, he only survived for seven years until 1982 when his heart finally gave up. Amazingly, it was decided that all government and Aramco employees were to be given an extra month's salary at this sad turn of events.

The official statement initially seemed to imply that this was because of the death of the king, but was eventually amended to state that it was in fact, a bonus to celebrate the installation of the new one. As employees, we were more than happy to receive a bonus whatever the reason, but it did seem a little odd at the time.

The concept of the crown passing down the line from one brother to the next invariably meant the succeeding monarch was barely any younger than the last. This elevation of geriatrics to the role of monarch would surely give rise to the payment of a bonus on a fairly regular basis... or so we hoped.

The new king was Fahd, the first of the so-called 'Sudairi Seven' to assume this role. King Abdulaziz's favourite wife had been Hussa bint Ahmed Al Sudairi, who had given him a total of seven sons. Fahd thus became the first of the 'Sudairi Seven' to be king, but most of his brothers would hold the key levers of power, in some cases right up until the present day.

Fahd needless to say, went on to live until 2005 and so during my time with the company, there were sadly, no further windfall bonuses.

Chapter 10

A Place of My Own

I lived in the temporary house on 16th Street for about eighteen months until I eventually accrued sufficient housing points to bid on some permanent housing. Although I had enjoyed my time in the temporary house and made some good friends, I wanted my wife to visit me occasionally and this would not be possible until I found permanent accommodation.

Housing was segregated into 'Family Housing' which were typically three, four or even five bedroomed dwellings and quite naturally reserved for those employees on family status with children. For someone on bachelor status like myself, there was a variety of dwellings available which had some rather strange names.

The smallest of these were called 'efficiencies' which everyone dubbed 'deficiencies', there were also 'windmills' - so named because they were four dwellings attached to each other which, from the air, allegedly resembled a windmill sail. Other types of houses were referred to by the square footage of each - there were '500 units', '670 units', '700 units' and '900 units'. Regardless of the size, they would typically be either one, or two storey, single bedroomed townhouses with a kitchen and reception room downstairs.

The method by which such moves were facilitated was via the housing list, posted every week in the mail centre. This list was in two parts; the available houses together with a description and location on one side and on the other, the list of people requiring permanent accommodation with their respective number of housing points. Employees would study these lists keenly to see what houses had become available and just as importantly, whether their housing points would be sufficient to give them a realistic chance of successfully bidding on any of them.

Grade code was a major factor in determining housing points and people could move up or down the list, as it was not solely related to length of service. If the company had recently hired a number of higher grade code employees, the existing employee might find him, or herself, lower down on the list than before. It made for exciting and often frustrating reading for employees seeking to move out of temporary accommodation, or indeed for employees who had been there a while, looking to find more expansive accommodation.

After weeks of looking, I eventually saw a two-storey, 700 square foot unit in Dhahran Hills which lay on the other side of the golf course from the older part of camp, where I had been living in the temporary house. It was exactly what I was looking for and might possibly be attainable even with my modest points tally and so I duly submitted my bid. I received a call from the housing office a week later and was informed that the house was mine and that I would be able to move in a couple of weeks' time after it had been cleaned and repainted.

Furniture - beds, sofas, tables and lamps etc. could be viewed and ordered at a notional rent from the company's furniture warehouse. There was also a choice of carpet colour as all permanent houses were completely re-carpeted every time a new occupier moved in. I visited the warehouse and made my various selections. Within a week I had the keys and completed the handover. At last I had a place of my own.

Dhahran Hills was a little different from the older part of camp. All the main facilities, the commissary, library, cinema and dining hall etc. were located in the older areas which was about half a mile away on the other side of the golf course. At that time I was still working at Dhahran North which meant that I was either picked up to go into work, or had the use of a company vehicle. Company vehicles were strictly for work use and were not supposed to be used in the evenings and at weekends and certainly not to be taken off camp unless for business reasons. I therefore felt that without my own means of transport, I might feel a little isolated. It was clearly time to buy a car.

I didn't really want to spend a lot of money as I intended to use it mainly on the camp. Transportation to local towns for shopping was in any case possible by using buses provided by the company. Many residents had what they called 'camp cars', often antique vehicles which were pretty much unroadworthy. You certainly wouldn't trust them on the main roads beyond the camp perimeter. I started looking on the 'For Sale' section of the notice board in the mail centre hoping that someone might be selling something of interest.

After a couple of weeks I saw a photograph of a small, silver Honda Civic. This would be perfect and in the photograph, it appeared to be in reasonably good condition considering that it was about six years old. I called the number attached to the photo and arranged a viewing and test drive. The owner was a Lebanese employee and we therefore had to go through a bit of haggling over the price. Eventually we reached a deal.

The car was great for getting around the camp and I would trust it just enough to occasionally drive the ten miles to the company's private beach at Half Moon Bay, or to the nearby city of Al Khobar.

Chapter 11

Party Central

Life in Saudi Arabia was nothing if not social. Work colleagues and other employees encountered through membership and participation in the various self-directed groups meant that it was possible to build up a wide social circle in a relatively short space of time. With no entertainment venues of any sort, socialising was done within Dhahran and more often than not, in the home. Apart from smaller gatherings, dinner parties and so on, for most young employees on bachelor status such as I, large and often rowdy parties were the feature of many weekends. Illicit home-made booze would flow freely and attendees would generally get hammered.

In larger homes, parties would often spill out into the gardens and sometimes into the swimming pool…..literally. I recall one particular party in the early eighties when an American friend decided that it would be a good idea to have a 'Beach Party'. He duly contacted the Community Services Department and asked them to lay plastic sheeting throughout his house and then deliver a large truckload of fine sand to be spread over the sheeting. Incredibly, they complied with this somewhat unusual request and duly transformed his house into a 'beach'. Dress code for the party of course, was swimming gear and flip flops.

It was a two-storey house although the sand beneath our feet was limited to the ground floor. One guest got so carried away with the beach theme and, under the influence of a little too much alcohol, went upstairs, found an ironing board and decided that it would be a good idea to 'surf' down the stairs. He received a loud ovation for this wonderfully themed display, but sadly broke his collar bone when his 'surfboard' reached the foot of the stairs and slammed him into the front door!

With typical efficiency, community services turned up the following day with some workmen and laboriously shovelled out all the sand, removed the plastic sheeting and restored the house to its original condition… all at the company's expense.

Some parties weren't always so successful. If they were very loud and perhaps some of the near neighbours had not been invited, there was a possibility that a complaint might be made to Industrial Security who would pay a visit. Industrial Security knew of course, that there would be alcohol on the premises and would usually just close the party down without too much fuss, but you could never be certain. I recall one party which was held for the cast of the Dhahran Theatre Group which had just completed a short run of *The Pirates of Penzance*. I wasn't involved in the Theatre Group, but knew a number of people who were and so found myself invited.

It was a hell of a party, but inevitably it went on very loudly and very late. Word got round that there had been complaints from some of the neighbours and that we were about to be raided by industrial security, or even the police. There followed an unseemly scramble to get out. I and a number of others found ourselves in the rear garden which was surrounded by quite high and smooth concrete walls.

Being somewhat inebriated, we attempted to scale the walls while onlookers hummed the signature tune of *The Great Escape*. Some took running jumps and succeeded in gripping the top of the wall, managing to pull themselves up so they could perch on the top and offer a hand to those below.

Others opted to climb onto another guest's shoulders in order to make their escape. I think about ten of us succeeded in making our getaway in this fashion although we learned later that industrial security had merely asked all the guests politely to leave and there had been no involvement of the outside police.

I mentioned the complete absence of places of entertainment outside of the Aramco camp where alcohol was available, but there was one legal exception to this rule. Next door to the United States consulate, which was situated on the perimeter of Dhahran Airport, was the 'Marine House', just a couple of miles from Dhahran. As with all US embassies and consulates, a detachment of US Marines was assigned to guard each facility.

The 'Marine House' was technically US soil and as a consequence, there was a bar where the off-duty marines could relax and entertain visitors. A good friend of mine was a former marine and was able to access this facility whenever he chose. He often invited me to accompany him and it was always great fun.

The marines enjoyed getting some of their guests drunk and then giving them a 'marine haircut'. Anyone who has seen the film *Jarheads* will know the look. I fortunately escaped this fate, but many a guest woke up the next day wondering why their heads had been shaved. Shaved heads were decidedly not a popular look in the eighties.

Drinking and driving were most definitely discouraged by the company, but many did it anyway, especially on camp and often while driving company vehicles. There were frequent accidents as a result, though these were rarely fatal as speed limits were extremely low and even drunken drivers would generally not drive so fast. A colleague of mine who was a seriously big drinker had driven late one night to a party being held in one of the temporary houses.

Largely constructed of wood, the house rested on a number of brick columns four feet off the ground. He had parked nose in to the house and as he clambered into his company car upon leaving, instead of engaging reverse on the automatic gearbox, he inadvertently engaged drive and pushed down on the accelerator. He promptly drove into the house, or more accurately into the supports holding up the house.

The brick supports at the front of the house gave way and the house, deprived of its full complement of supporting columns, lurched forward and came to rest on the bonnet of the intruding car. The car was stuck and no amount of drunken revving and engaging of the reverse gear was going to change anything. Aware that the misuse of company vehicles, especially while under the influence of alcohol, was a termination offence, my colleague decided he had only one course of action......to leg it.

He knew of course, even in his befuddled state that there would come a reckoning. The car was assigned to him and he knew that the following morning, Industrial Security would be beating a path to his door. By then he would at least be sober and able to gather his thoughts to find some semi-plausible explanation for exactly how he had managed to park his car under a house.

Somehow he managed to talk his way out of it and amazingly received only a reprimand for his misdeed. When the tow truck arrived the following day to pull the car out, part of the house for which it had been providing temporary support, duly collapsed.

Chapter 12

Getting The Chop

Executions were a fact of life in Saudi Arabia. Public beheadings took place after midday prayers on Fridays in towns and cities up and down the country. The executions were regularly announced on the Saudi news channels and were not at all concealed, indeed they were celebrated as the will of God being carried out and also to serve as a warning to anyone who might be contemplating a criminal act.

Executions were normally reserved for cases of murder, terrorism, or drug smuggling. Less serious offences such as repetitive convictions for theft would be dealt with by the severing of hands, or a spell in prison. Executions in the Eastern Province were usually held in the provincial capital of Dammam, about five miles north of Dhahran. After prayers, the condemned would be brought to an open area behind the main mosque which we expatriates irreverently named 'Chop Chop Square'.

I never personally attended one of these executions, but knew a few expatriates who had. Indeed when the local onlookers became aware of their presence, they were pushed to the front so they might obtain a better view. One of them later recounted that a spray of blood from the victim had landed on his shoes.

The usual procedure was that the convicted man would arrive in the back of a police pickup truck, bound and hooded. Large crowds of locals would form a circle around the executioner holding a large, curved sword and waiting patiently for his next victim.

The condemned man would be heavily sedated, though still able to stand. The hood would be removed and he would kneel in the sand in front of the executioner, hands bound behind his back. A few prayers would be uttered before the silver sword swirled around and came down, severing the head with one blow.

Polite applause would ring out among the assembled onlookers, in appreciation that God's will had been done. The head and body would then be wrapped in a large sheet and thrown into the back of the pick-up truck before being driven away. Show over, the crowd would disperse.

I recall reading a press cutting from the time regarding executions. One of the older executioners, named Abu Sayyaf (Father of the Sword) had given an interview. He claimed to have performed over six hundred beheadings during his long career which he had evidently enjoyed. He went on to say that he preferred beheadings to hand amputations as the removal of a hand required greater care because the victim would survive the ordeal and the cut needed to be precise.

Abu Sayyaf said that he was paid a very modest monthly salary with an additional bonus payment of two hundred dollars per head. 'I always look forward to the opportunity to chop off more heads so that I can earn more money' he was quoted as saying.

He said that on one occasion he had to behead two criminals at the same time and that they were both kneeling on the sand. He swung his sword down on the neck of the first victim, whose severed head fell directly in front of the second man causing him to collapse on the ground and die of a heart attack.

He went on to say that on the rare occasion he had to execute a woman, he would use a pistol rather than carry out a beheading with his sword. Using his sword would have required him to remove the woman's clothing from around the neck and shoulders which would have been an affront to her modesty. I seriously doubted whether the poor woman would have been too concerned about this at the time.

Medieval and barbaric it may seem to us, but it was an everyday fact of life. As far as the locals were concerned, it was merely the carrying out of God's will and not really a topic for debate. I was aware that these things took place on a fairly regular basis and only a few miles from where I was living, but confess I never gave it much further thought.

It must be said that the severe punishments for criminal behaviour did make for a virtually crime-free environment. In those days people often left their cars unlocked and frequently carried large sums of cash. The company's Saudi employees routinely received their entire monthly salary in cash. If you went into the bank in Dhahran on a pay day you would watch in amazement as employees stuffed huge wads of bank notes into supermarket bags before carrying them off without any concern.

Chapter 13

Coast to Coast - A Trip to the Red Sea

*E*id al Adha*, or the 'Feast of the Sacrifice' is one of the most important events in the Islamic calendar. It commemorates Abraham offering to sacrifice his son Isaac - Ishmael in Arabic. It is a story also contained in the Old Testament of the bible and the time that millions of Muslims make the pilgrimage to Mecca.

The *haj* pilgrimage is one of the five pillars of Islam and should be undertaken at least once in a lifetime by the true believer. Every year, Muslims from around the world make the often long and arduous trip to Mecca and then on to Medina to visit the Prophet's Mosque, the final resting place of the Prophet Mohammed and the second holiest site in Islam after Mecca.

Eid al Adha was also a national holiday and all company employees would get five days off work. I was not due a vacation and it looked as though I would be spending the five day period engaged in a number of sporting and drinking activities, until a friend mentioned that he was minded to hire a car and drive across the Arabian peninsula and back during the five day holiday for 'a bit of a laugh'.

The Arabian peninsula is approximately one thousand miles from the Gulf coast to the Red Sea, so it was not a journey to be taken lightly. There was a little bit of planning involved, but in reality not too much. Eventually myself and three other like-minded souls bought into the idea.

A dark red Chevrolet Impala was duly hired, and camp beds were bought or borrowed. There would be no need for tents as the evening temperature at that time of year would never drop below twenty-five degrees Celsius The camp beds were more to avoid the nocturnal attentions of scorpions and snakes rather than for comfort.

We set off in the early morning and initially took the Abqaiq Highway which led from Dhahran to the south west. Abqaiq was Aramco's main oil processing facility and the second largest community after Dhahran. After Abqaiq came Ain Dar, which translated as 'abode of the eye' in Arabic, little more than a road junction. The road then turned due west in the direction of Riyadh.

These days, major roads in Saudi Arabia are six and often eight-lane highways, but in the eighties the road from Dhahran to Riyadh was an ordinary two lane highway and to say that you took your life in your hands on such a road was an understatement. Heavy and often overladen trucks, frequently operated by inexperienced drivers from the third world, competed for road space with local drivers whose chief ambition was to scare any oncoming traffic off the road.

On the approach to Riyadh from the east, the sand suddenly changes colour. Just beyond Khurais, the dull grey-brown sand of the Eastern Province gives way to the bright orange sand of the Najd desert. Even in those days, there was a rudimentary ring road around the capital and, conscious of the limited time available to cross and re-cross the Arabian peninsula in just five days, we determined that a fuller investigation of all that the city had to offer would have to wait for another occasion.

Heading now to the north west, the sun was already low on the western horizon by the time we reached a suitably remote location for our campsite. Pulling onto hard-packed sand we moved far enough away from the road to avoid any nocturnal traffic collisions and parked in the shelter of some rocky outcrops. Camp beds were erected and a small gas stove was lit to prepare an evening delicacy of baked beans and beef sausages. We lined up the camp beds very close to the car to afford some protection should the wind get up during the night and also to allow us to seek the protection of the vehicle should we be bothered by wild dogs.

Until you have experienced night in the desert with a cloudless sky and no moon, far away from city lights, it is difficult to describe the infinite array of stars visible above. As we lay on our camp beds in the silent desert, shooting stars and the occasional satellite were the only things that moved among the heavenly host twinkling above our heads. Had it not been my weariness after spending eight hours on the road, I'm sure I would not have slept, so wonderful was the sight.

Dawn comes swiftly in those latitudes and the sun was already above the horizon when we awoke at six. Mugs of coffee and bowls of cereal were quickly consumed before we began the second day of our trip, by the end of which we hoped to be close to the Red Sea. It would turn out to be a long and eventful day.

Our immediate destination was the oasis town of Buraydah. Almost exactly equidistant from the Arabian Gulf and the Red Sea, it would have been impossibly remote until recent times, accessible only by camel train. Saudi Arabia in 1979 was very much a work in progress. The wealth that oil had brought was only just beginning to be spent on infrastructure. Buraydah had a main road and it had street lights, but that was about all.

Flat roofed houses huddled alongside narrow alleyways leading off the road and although there were some vehicles, donkeys and camels were the preferred form of transport. It was like returning to biblical times. The old town was surrounded by date palm groves and small orchards of lemon and orange trees. The basis of its economy and the reason the town existed, was due to the life sustaining presence of fresh water. At the local petrol station, we managed not only to fill the car, but load up with a few supplies of food including some hot *shawarmas*.

After Buraydah, the road turned due west and after about thirty miles the orange red sand of the Najd gave way to an increasingly rocky and hilly topography. We were driving into the foothills of the Hijaz mountains, the spine of which runs all the way down the western side of the Arabian peninsula from the Jordanian border in the north, to Yemen in the south.

The hills gradually became mountains as the road snaked through wadis and ravines, climbing ever higher with each turn. Gone were the heavy commercial vehicles which had made the roads busy and dangerous all the way to and around the outskirts of Riyadh, the trucks now replaced by buses crammed with pilgrims headed for the holy cities of Mecca and Medina.

It was after all, the festival of *Eid Al Adha*, when hundreds of thousands of devout Muslims descend upon these places to perform the annual *haj*. While these days many arrive by air, or by sea landing at Jeddah, in former times the only way the faithful could travel was by camel train. Those with limited income would now travel by bus, not only from within Saudi Arabia, but from countries such as Kuwait, Iraq, Jordan, Syria and Iran.

These pilgrim buses were a sight to behold. Antique and gaily painted, filled with pilgrims wearing only *ihram* clothing which consisted of two sheets of white, towelling material. Luggage as well as some hardy passengers, clung onto racks which ran along the roof of the bus.

In later years I would travel extensively throughout the third world where such sights are the norm, but I had never seen the like before. We passed dozens of these venerable and over-loaded vehicles as we snaked our way up into the mountains. The sound of chanting came through the open windows of the non-air conditioned buses. It resembled some kind of weird works outing where instead of having a sing-song and quaffing bottles of beer, they were reciting and chanting verses from the Qur'an.

Ever conscious of time, we were easily able to overtake these lumbering antiques as they struggled up the steep inclines, belching smoke into the hot Arabian sky. The sun descended ever lower into the western sky ahead and by late afternoon we were approaching Medina, the second holiest city in Islam. There are many holy cities in Islam, some recognised only by the Shia sect and others universally acknowledged by all Muslims. The three holiest are Mecca, Medina and Jerusalem, or Al Quds as it is known in Arabia.

Mecca is the birthplace of the prophet Mohammed and the site of the grand mosque which encloses the *Kaaba*, a black granite structure considered by Muslims to be the *Bayt Allah*, or

House of God. It is the direction, or *qiblah* towards which the faithful must always face when performing their daily prayers. The square building is covered in an elaborately embroidered cloth and in one corner, set in a silver surround, is a black stone, thought to be a meteorite. The faithful will circumambulate the *Kaaba* seven times and will try, though most usually fail, to get close enough to kiss the black stone.

Medina, termed Al Madinah in Arabic simply means 'city'. It was known as Yathrib in the prophet's time and it was the city to which he fled for sanctuary after being hounded out of Mecca. This is the so-called *Hijrah*, or flight and the date is Year 1 in the Islamic calendar. The prophet is buried in the majestic *Masjid al Nabawi* in the centre of the city.

We were well aware that Medina was strictly off-limits to non-Muslims, but we had also been advised before setting off on our journey that a well-signposted bypass would take us around the city on the northern side from where we could continue our journey onward to the coast. In the late afternoon, we drove steadily in the direction of the setting sun. We passed a few buildings as we headed towards the city, ever mindful that we needed to pick up a sign for the ring road, or 'heathen bypass' as we non-Muslims called it.

Buildings became more frequent and still there was no sign. We debated the fact that we may have missed it and whether or not we should turn round and retrace our route. John, who had taken over driving duties for that sector, was confident that we had not missed any sign and proceeded onwards. The minarets and domes of the large mosques in the city centre were getting ever closer before we finally decided that we must have missed the turn.

Deciding to make a U-turn at the next set of traffic lights, we were dismayed to see a policeman stationed there. He looked into the car as we stopped and our hearts sank. He motioned for us to go no further and got onto his radio, launching into a stream of Arabic. At first he didn't seem sure of what to do, but as the lights had changed to green, he motioned for us to do a U turn and pull up at the side of the road facing the opposite direction.

Within minutes we were surrounded by four police cars and asked to produce our identification - in our case passports and *iqamas* (resident permits). None of the police seemed to speak any English and John tried to explain in rudimentary Arabic that we had got lost and missed the turn-off. Much chatter on radios followed while we remained seated in the car. I looked out of the back window and could clearly see the green dome of the prophet's mosque less than half a mile away. Eventually, by use of sign language, we were instructed to follow a police car away from the city centre with two cars following on behind us.

We followed the police car to a lay-by on the outskirts of the city, where we were instructed to hand over our passports. These were taken away by another police car back in the direction of the city. My dreams of completing two years employment seemed to be evaporating in to the hot Arabian air as we speculated about the likely punishment we might receive for such an awful transgression. Although the policemen spoke little English, they were not aggressive and were quite polite. As we were now beyond the limits of the holy *haram* we were allowed out of the car to stretch our legs.

By this time the sun was going down and all of the policemen left to go and pray by the side of the road. A large four wheel drive then pulled in behind us accompanied by a police car. We walked over to the car as we could see it contained two couples who turned out to be American expats and fellow Aramco employees. They had made the same mistake as we had and had been detained when approaching the city centre. The ladies seemed a little distressed and they told us what had happened. They had been arrested and rather than being escorted back out to the city limits as we had, had driven under escort to the main police station in the centre of the city, just across from the *Masjid al Nabawi*. The men were taken inside while the women were left in the vehicle.

The sight of two western ladies in a vehicle parked in the very centre of Medina, naturally caused some interest from the locals and quite soon a large crowd had congregated by the car. One of the ladies thought that it might be an idea to wind down her window and engage in conversation with some of the small boys, perhaps to defuse the situation before it possibly turned hostile. One of the boys who spoke a little English said to her, 'you shouldn't be here.' She said that she knew that, but had merely made a mistake. She asked him what he thought would happen now to which he smiled sweetly, then made a cutting sign with his hand across his throat.

At that point she swiftly wound up the window and prayed that the men would re-join them as soon as possible. They eventually reappeared, and under police escort drove to the same lay-by as we found ourselves in. After a further half hour wait, by which time it was dark, a police car containing the captain, arrived back from the city with all our passports.

We gathered around him as he handed each of us our passports. He reminded us that as non-Muslims we were not allowed to enter the holy city of Medina, but he realised it was a genuine mistake and he would instruct one of his policeman lead us on the correct road around the city. It was quite late by the time we left our police escort and headed west to find another campsite for the night. We were so exhausted by our brush with the authorities that we needed no help sleeping. At least I would be able to say that I was one of the few non-Muslims to have seen the Prophet's Mosque.

We camped that night in the mountains and the next morning dawned calm and clear. We estimated that we would cover the remaining distance to the Red Sea by lunchtime, but still had to ascend the highest ridge. When we got to the crest, the view was impressive, the black basalt mountains stretching away into the distance. We were only forty miles away from the coast, but the coastal haze hid it from view.

We were now on the downhill run and continued to pass a motley collection of vehicles with their inevitable load of white clad pilgrims. Here and there flocks of sheep and goats appeared among the rocky landscape. It was hard to see any vegetation at all among the jagged and desolate landscape, but there must have been something out there for them to eat. Our run down the western side of the mountains was uneventful and at last we saw the sun reflecting off the blue waters of the Red Sea.

Our immediate destination was Yanbu, formerly a fishing village in which a young T.E. Lawrence - Lawrence of Arabia - had briefly stayed during the Arab Revolt as he made his way northwards towards Jordan and Syria. I thought it a little odd that there were few, if any references to either Lawrence, or the Arab revolt in modern day Saudi Arabia. I discovered that this was due to the fact that up until 1926 the Hijaz was a separate kingdom ruled by the Al Hashem dynasty. This was the family who had provided support and soldiers to Lawrence in order to oust the Turks who had dominated Arabia for more than a hundred years.

The Al Saud at that time were located in the isolated backwater of Riyadh and played no role in the revolt. At the conclusion of the First World War, the Al Hashem would be rewarded with Transjordan then under British Mandate and the reason why to this day, it is formally known as the Hashemite Kingdom of Jordan.

It was some years later that King Abdulaziz Al Saud unified the greater part of the Arabian peninsula into what is today known as Saudi Arabia, therefore references to the Al Hashem, or indeed to what was formerly the Kingdom of Hijaz, have been expunged from the history books.

Under the auspices of the Royal Commission, Yanbu was being rapidly transformed from a small fishing village into an industrial city. Aramco was in the process of building an export refinery and gas plant which would eventually handle the crude oil received from the East-West pipeline currently under construction. This project would reduce Saudi Arabia's dependence on ships passing through the Straits of Hormuz and allow it to export oil regardless of potential political problems in the Gulf.

Some old buildings of the town, their balconies covered by wooden lattices still existed, but they were disappearing fast. I visited Yanbu some years later and sadly found that the remainder had been swept away in the relentless pursuit of modernity. After a brief stop we continued our journey south along the coast road which would lead to Jeddah.

On the way we passed through Rabigh which was still a small fishing port on a sheltered lagoon. Thankfully it had thus far escaped the attentions of industrial development and probably looked the same as Yanbu had just five years earlier. The old houses with their distinctive balconies huddled by the seashore while around the lagoon, an inviting sandy beach enticed us for a dip in the crystal clear, warm waters of the Red Sea.

We made camp that night on the seashore and went to sleep not only with the wondrous vista of stars, but also the gentle crash of waves upon the shore. Heavenly.

The following morning we were up with the sun, broke camp and after a hasty breakfast headed south down the coast to Jeddah, the largest city in Saudi Arabia. It only took an hour to reach the outskirts and we drove into the centre, parked the car and went on foot. There were some old buildings to be seen, but clearly most had been torn down and replaced by ugly, modern blocks. I wondered if at some point in the future, the Saudis might regret losing these buildings in the insane quest for modernity.

'Modernity' also included western fast-food restaurants including a McDonald's to which we made our way for a cooked breakfast. Obviously pork was off the menu, but in all other respects it was just like any other McDonald's the world over. Our hunger satisfied, we continued our exploration on foot. It was about half an hour later that John realised that he had lost his passport. We had all taken our passports with us on the journey in accordance with the advice given by Aramco government affairs that if you were travelling outside of the Eastern Province, you should always take your passport because police had numerous checkpoints along the roads. These were evident at all times of the year, but especially so during the Hajj when hundreds of thousands of foreigners entered the kingdom. Security was always an obsession with the authorities.

We retraced our footsteps to McDonald's, but there was no sign of the missing passport. At that time, the British Embassy and most other foreign embassies were located in Jeddah, so we made our way there only to find it closed because of the holiday. Fortunately, there was a guard on the gate and we explained the problem. He summoned security from within the embassy compound and a helpful British employee came out to see us. He listened to what we had to say and informed us that all consular staff were currently on holiday. He did say however, that we would have to report the loss to the local police before any consular assistance could be provided.

He provided directions to the main police station. By this time it was late afternoon on the day of the sacrifice when thousands of sheep, goats and camels would be slaughtered in accordance with religious custom. We found the police station - a fairly run down building in the downtown area. We went inside and discovered a group of policemen busily slaughtering a goat in the stairwell, the pathetic bleats of the trussed and dying animal echoing down the blood soaked corridor.

None of the policemen spoke a word of English, but we were invited into the captain's office. What was evidently the captain's desk was positioned on a large dais about a foot higher than the floor level. We sat down on the small chairs opposite the dais and waited. About ten minutes later a small stocky individual entered the room, smiled at us and took his seat at the desk. A tray of hot, sweet tea in small glasses was duly brought in for him and for us.

He smiled at us while John explained the nature of our predicament. He listened politely then asked John to repeat what he had said, but in Arabic. We had only been in Saudi Arabia a relatively short time, so knew little Arabic beyond being able to exchange pleasantries. John however, to his credit, had been studying Arabic in the evenings since his arrival and he was able, haltingly to explain himself. The captain beamed with pleasure and although I'm sure he could speak reasonably good English, he chose to conduct the meeting entirely in Arabic, all the while idly spinning his revolver on the desk.

At last he professed himself satisfied with the story and more pertinently that he was satisfied that he had demonstrated to us that he was a man of power and at that moment, we were completely under his control. He proceeded to write a letter which would allow us to pass unhindered through any police roadblocks which we may encounter on our journey back to the Eastern Province. It later transpired that John's passport had been found and handed in to the police a few days later.

Time was marching on and we had only two more days in which to complete our journey. We took the Mecca road east out of the bustling city and it began to gradually ascend from the flat coastal plain into the foothills of the Hijaz. The black rocky crags became more apparent the higher we climbed. Conscious of our recent incident in Medina, we were relieved to see modern highways, clearly signposted with routes to be taken for non-Muslims, effectively a ring road around the outer extremities of the holy city. Mecca lies in a dry valley among the rugged Hijaz mountains, but the bypass took us away from the city, ever higher into the mountains towards Taif, summer capital of the royal family.

Eventually reaching Taif, we parked up a few hundred yards away from what appeared to be the royal summer palace resplendent with a brightly coloured dome. The air was refreshingly cool as we strolled around and took a break. We had reached the highest point of the Hijaz at this latitude, which was over six thousand feet. The range continued southwards for another thousand miles into Yemen where it reached its highest altitude of over twelve-thousand feet. I had heard that the mountains there were green and lush all year round on account of the frequent rainfall. I would have to test that theory another time.

Time was passing by and we needed to cover a few more miles before sundown. With the setting sun behind us we pulled off the road onto some hard-packed sand and made camp for the night.

The sun rose on cue the following morning at six. We had a hasty breakfast and hit the road once again as we needed to reach Dhahran that day and had many miles to cover. We had driven a short distance across the featureless desert terrain, when we saw two figures in Arab dress standing by the road. They flagged us down and we stopped. It was a very elderly man accompanied presumably by his son, or grandson. Their English was minimal, but we gradually gathered that the old man required a lift. The time honoured code of the desert is hospitality and assistance to those in need, so we agreed to take the old man further along the road to the east.

It seemed that the elderly man could barely see through his rheumy eyes, but after we had travelled twenty miles or so, he banged on the dashboard and shouted *Hinna* (here).

We slowed the car and looked around the bleak landscape for some sign of habitation, but there was none. The old man was however insistent that this was his destination, so he got out and hobbled slowly away across the sand. We looked at each other in amazement - where on earth was he headed?

We decided that it was really none of our business and we drove off, having performed our good deed for the day. We eventually pulled into the Aramco compound at Dhahran late in the evening of the last day of the holiday. The two-thousand mile trip, completed in just five days had certainly been an adventure.

Chapter 14

Getting in Shape

When I shared a temporary house on the main camp with two keen runners, it was almost inevitable that I would start to join in. I had never really been into athletics, interminable cross country runs in cold and wet conditions during my schooldays had put paid to that, but with lots of free time, warm weather and a new-found desire to keep fit, I began to run.

Among the plethora of self-directed groups, there existed a road runners club which organised a number of races and social events during the cooler winter months. It could never be said that the company failed to provide facilities for most sports and that included athletics. There were two floodlit all-weather running tracks available, each with immaculate surfaces that would have been the envy of prestigious athletics club anywhere in the world. So it was that I became a member of the Dhahran Road Runners Club.

I recall the first time I went running with my housemates. Kitted out in some inappropriate old pumps and even more inappropriate tight shorts, we headed for the nearest running track, about half a mile from the house. I had anticipated a leisurely stroll down, a bit of running then a stroll back, but to my surprise, my housemates immediately broke into a jog as soon as we left the house.

After a few visits to the track, a run in the relative cool of the evenings soon became the norm. Struggling to complete four laps initially, my distances gradually increased over the next few months. I eventually bought some proper running shoes and began to take my running more seriously.

Throughout the cooler winter months, the running club would put on a variety of races, typically of five and ten kilometres, in addition to half and full marathons. Barely three months after I had started running, a ten kilometre run seemed nothing out of the ordinary and was completed with relative ease. I was never particularly fast and although my times were respectable, I knew that I could never beat any of the good runners over shorter distances. Endurance however was another matter and, in my late twenties, I felt as though I could run forever.

I would put this theory to the test when I completed my first half marathon. Aching, but elated, I was persuaded by one of my friends that I should enter the full Dhahran marathon which was to take place in a few weeks' time. The twenty six mile course would start from the company's private beach at Half Moon Bay, up to Dhahran and back again.

Setting off in darkness, I completed the outward thirteen mile section in reasonably good order, but the return to the beach was an altogether different proposition. As I passed the twenty mile marker, my legs increasingly felt like lead and my pace already slow, began to get even slower. Just six miles to go I told myself, but it might as well have been sixty miles.

At the twenty two mile marker, my legs stopped functioning

completely and I was unable to put one foot in front of the other. I sat down in the road, tears of anger and frustration welling up as the realisation dawned that I had bitten off more than I could chew. Rather than vowing never to do it again, I decided that I would complete a marathon, but that next time I would prepare properly. Never again would I have to sit down in the middle of the road in tears. It's not a pretty sight to see a grown man cry.

I went on to complete many marathons over the following twenty years, but always prepared thoroughly and was always confident of finishing. The image of sitting on that lonely road in the middle of the desert, unable to put one leg in front of the other always stayed with me as a motivational force.

The great thing about the company was that they would bend over backwards to keep their employees happy, this extended to the financial and practical support given to self-directed groups. The running club was no exception, although in truth we needed very little in terms of support. There was one glorious occasion however, which sticks in my mind.

As mentioned before, there were a number of other company towns scattered across the Eastern Province, Ras Tanura and Safaniyah in the north and Abqaiq and Udhailiyah in the south. Each had its own community and self-directed groups, although these were on a much smaller scale than Dhahran.

Udhailiyah was about 150 miles south of Dhahran and quite a journey by road at that time. A number of company pilots were keen runners and when the Udhailiyah running club, with a membership of only around fifty, decided to organise a road race, we thought it might be fun to enter. It might at least provide a change of scenery. They had invited runners from Dhahran and other company communities, so some of the pilots sought the Aramco Aviation Department's approval for some transportation assistance.

The assistance turned out to be a company Boeing 737 no less, which would fly the thirty interested runners from Dhahran and Ras Tanura down to Udhailiyah. So it was that we turned up in our tracksuits one Friday morning at the company hangar, boarded the aircraft which took off, initially flying to Ras Tanura, a fifteen minute flight. It landed at the small airstrip to pick up the handful of runners and then took off once again for Udhailyah, a twenty minute flight. After the race, the aircraft repeated its journey, dropping the six residents of Ras Tanura off, before flying once more into Dhahran with the remaining thirty runners.

All these years later it still seems incredible that a company would provide a jet airliner to transport a handful of people on such a trivial recreational jaunt. The term 'money no object' doesn't even begin to cover it.

Chapter 15

A Very Saudi Wedding

It is a well-publicised fact that in Islam, a man is permitted to have up to four wives. Arabs, I discovered, tend to have a public life and a private one and only when you got to know one really well, would you perhaps be permitted a glimpse into his private life.

The origins of this custom are not quite as salacious as many would like to believe. Due to the severe restrictions on how females can conduct themselves in public, it is very difficult for them to carry out any business which would bring them into contact with a man. The father, husband or indeed the son, if he is old enough, will therefore perform these duties on behalf of the woman.

In the event that a woman has no father, or husband it would be natural for her to enter into a marriage regardless of whether the man was already be married, in order to live under his protection. It was not unusual for a widow to marry her brother-in-law for this reason, even though he might already have a wife.

Many of the younger generation appear to be adopting a more monogamous lifestyle however. Western influences do indeed penetrate the kingdom via television and other media and many younger women would not tolerate their husbands marrying a second, third, or even a fourth wife even though legally they would have no way of preventing it.

Should a man seek to marry more than one wife, he is required under Islam to treat all his wives fairly and equally, providing all of them with the same material and emotional comforts. This could turn out to be a tremendously expensive enterprise and these days is usually the preserve of the very wealthy.

While one would hesitate to ask about a man's marital arrangements, it was quite natural to ask about his children, particularly his sons. One of the most touching aspects of Arab culture is their love of children and the more the merrier.

I had been married for over ten years before my daughter was born, which occasioned a measure of disbelief among my Saudi friends and colleagues. Saudis typically started families just as soon as they were married and they must have thought there was something wrong with me. So concerned was one of my young Saudi colleagues, he decided to bring me some dates every morning, insisting that they were a certain remedy to improve my evident lack of potency. Dates are not my favourite thing, but not wishing to cause offence, I would chew them while he made crude hand gestures to emphasise his point.

Having a family is such a vital part of the Arab culture that men are often referred to by close friends and family, not by their given name, but by the honorific title of father - *Abu* in Arabic of whatever the name of their eldest son happened to be. If a man's eldest son was Mohammed, he would therefore be referred to as Abu Mohammed. For a mother it was the same, she would be referred to as mother - *Umm* in Arabic and so be referred to as Umm Mohammed. Only in cases where there were no male offspring would the honorific titles of *Abu* and *Umm* be used in conjunction with the eldest daughter's name.

One of my running friends, who was in his late twenties and quite old for a Saudi getting married for the first time, was organising his wedding. My wife who was visiting me at the time and I, received an invitation to the wedding. Marriage ceremonies in Saudi Arabia and indeed in much of the Muslim world are quite informal. The 'wedding' to which guests are invited is basically what we would term the reception, a time for friends and family to meet the bride and groom. This being Arabia things happened a little differently and it would very much depend upon whether you were a male or female guest as to whether you would meet the bride or the groom... you would certainly not meet both.

If not held in a private home or in a large hotel, receptions are often held in what are known as 'Wedding Palaces' which can be found in towns and cities across the land. They are typically two storey affairs with vehicle access to the ground floor, but with a vehicle ramp curving up to the first floor. The reason for this is that there are two wedding receptions, one for the bride and the female guests and one on the top floor for the groom and his guests.

And so it was that my wife went in the downstairs door while I and the other male guests went into the upper floor. The host, his father and brothers made us most welcome. There was an array of food laid out on the huge carpet in the centre of the vast room with trays of dates, cakes and various sweetmeats.

Servants came around with *oudh,* a strong perfume in a type of incense burner and we were invited to waft some of the powerful fragrance onto ourselves. Tiny cups of coffee and tea were poured from a great height out of enormous coffee and tea pots.

A group of musicians sat in one corner of the room playing typical Arabic music and it wasn't long before we were invited up to dance. A room full of men dancing with each other, many wearing long white 'dresses' was something I never thought I'd see, much less participate in.

Eventually there was a break in the music and we resumed our sitting positions, cross-legged on the carpets while servants brought in the main course which was the traditional festive meal of *khabsa*. This is basically a whole roasted goat, lamb or even a camel laid upon a vast mound of rice.

We all dug in with our right hands - the left hand being considered unclean - shoving handfuls of rice and goat into our mouths. After the food was demolished it was time for more dancing. There was of course no alcohol served at this function, but there was plenty of tea, coffee and a variety of iced soft drinks.

At around ten o'clock, the groom and his brother bade fare-wells to their male guests and headed downstairs to join the bride. They were the only two men permitted this honour. The male party gradually dissolved after this, although there were still mounds of food available on the various trays spread around the room.

My wife, who was in the ladies' party on the ground floor, later recounted the story of the quite different wedding that she had attended.

All the women had arrived dressed in black from head to toe, but after entering the hall and checking that no men were in the room, shed their *habiyahs* revealing exquisite, jewelled ball gowns, many bearing famous designer labels. Once a light meal, served by women, had been consumed, the music began and so did the dancing.

She was quite surprised at the erotic nature of the dancing, especially by the younger women. Some of the older ladies however, neither danced, or at any point removed their *habiyahs*. Some did not reveal their faces which remained hidden behind black leather masks, their hands sheathed in black gloves.

When the bridegroom and his brother, entered the hall there was a flurry of veils being re-attached and the covering of hair. Only the bride remained uncovered, standing by her new husband and listening attentively as he made a short speech to all the ladies present. Formalities over, it was time for the happy couple to leave and the celebrations draw to a close.

Chapter 16

A Free Press

In addition to the wealth of Arabic language publications, two English language newspapers were produced in Saudi Arabia, the *Saudi Gazette* and the *Arab News*. The outer pages of the *Arab News* were printed on green paper and had been given the nickname among expatriates of 'The Green Truth'.

Although newspapers from the UK and other parts of the world were available, they typically only arrived in the shops five or six days after publication. Many expatriates would therefore pick up copies of these local papers, which at least contained some current news. Local news was fairly anodyne and nothing critical of either the government, or its policies would find its way into print. Foreign news on the other hand would be reported in a more robust way.

I often wondered whether a representative from the Ministry of Information sat on an editorial committee, but thought it more likely that editors received their guidelines when they were appointed. Apart from domestic and foreign news together with some social commentaries and sport, both of these newspapers devoted many column inches to religion, chiefly Islam.

I think these articles were mainly directed at the many

Muslims from the Indian sub-continent who were working in Saudi Arabia, but could not read Arabic. It may also have been a way of promoting Islam to non-believers and if this was the intent, then it failed spectacularly.

The religious pages often contained a 'readers letters' section in which people either asked for guidance on certain matters, or offered advice themselves. As a non-Muslim, I found it remarkable the degree to which Islam was involved with the minutiae of everyday life; how food should be prepared, how to wash and even how to use the bathroom.

These letter pages inevitably provided rich pickings for those with a mischievous sense of humour. Guessing that the editorial staff were probably not native English speakers and therefore not fully conversant with western terminology, they had their fun.

I recall one such letter, ostensibly written in reference to an earlier article in the paper about speech defects. The writer claimed that recent developments in this field had achieved a remarkable degree of success. It went on to say that these studies had been led by a certain Dr Linda Lovelace in the United States and involved a certain type of deep throat therapy. The letter was signed; I. Suckett of Jeddah!

A further letter asked in all apparent innocence whether it was permissible in Islam to have sexual intercourse with an animal, specifically in this case a goat. If the letter was amusing, the reply was hilarious. It stated that while it was not necessarily contrary to the laws of Islam to have sexual intercourse with a goat, it would not be deemed acceptable to eat it afterwards!

The late availability of foreign newspapers and magazines was due to two factors, the time taken to fly them into the kingdom and the time taken to censor them. The authorities must have employed armies of people to perform this task and I always carried a mental image of thousands of workers armed with felt-tipped pens and scissors wading through mountains of newspapers and magazines in some vast warehouse, obliterating and cutting out anything deemed offensive.

Censored items ranged from anything critical of government policies, human rights abuses, or indeed anything which could be considered embarrassing to the Saudi government. The chief concern however, seemed to be photographs, particularly those contained in magazines which included any scantily clad females. The army of censors, wielding their felt-tipped pens and probably themselves starved of female company, must have found the process of inking over pictures of female flesh a bittersweet process.

Chapter 17

Taking to the Water

With its headquarters in Dhahran, close to the shores of the Arabian Gulf, the company had its own private beach and yacht club at Half Moon Bay. Entry to the beach was restricted to employees and their families, while membership of the yacht club was dependent upon owning a registered boat. Many employees had boats, some were power boats, but most were typically catamarans, small mono-hulled yachts, or windsurfers.

The beach was the place to head at the weekends, either for walks along the sand, or to splash around in the crystal clear and usually very warm waters of the bay. The bay was virtually landlocked and stretched almost thirty miles to the opposite shore and the incredibly saline water was rarely rough. In true Saudi style there were many rules; all craft had to be removed from the water by sundown and each vessel, including windsurfers, was required to have a name and a coastguard registration number.

The Arabian Gulf is a very shallow sea, at its deepest point it is only three hundred feet deep and within the confines of Half Moon Bay it was no deeper than fifty feet. Despite the sandy bottom and virtual lack of coral, or marine vegetation, a surprising variety of marine life existed. Crustaceans, fish, dolphins and even the occasional dugong called this place home.

It was an ideal place to learn to sail, or scuba dive. I decided to do both. The notice board in the mail centre was the place to look for anyone wishing to buy just about anything, so when I saw an advertisement for a fairly antique windsurfer, it seemed the ideal craft on which to learn.

I duly bought it and then, with the assistance of the secretary of the yacht club, began the process of registering it with the appropriate authorities. This involved choosing a new name for it and so my new 'vessel' was given the unimaginative name of 'Waverider'.

A couple of weeks later the paperwork duly arrived which included a registration certificate which must be kept on board at all times the craft was in the water. Clearly the coastguards were not familiar with the complete lack of any watertight space on a windsurfer.

The yacht club secretary assured me that as long as the registration certificate was kept in my car when I was using the windsurfer, then it wouldn't be a problem. As a fit and healthy thirty two year old, I found windsurfing to be more strenuous than I had anticipated. The windsurfer was an old model and fairly large and cumbersome, but it was far more stable than some of the later models. Though ideal for learning, the size and weight of the sail made it very difficult to manoeuvre and should the sail fall in the water, it was extremely difficult to pull it back to the upright position.

Needless to say, I spent a great of time falling into the water, but the sea was like a lukewarm bath during the summer months, so it was no great hardship. After a few weekends when I spent more or less all the daylight hours at the beach, I gradually mastered the art of gybing and tacking and felt reasonably confident enough to venture further away from the beach. It was an exhilarating experience to catch the wind and pull on the bar, leaning backwards to gain maximum speed over the crystal waters of the Gulf and the antique surfboard began to live up to its name.

Occasional glimpses of marine life as I skimmed across the waves made me curious about what might live underwater. There were a couple of dive clubs in Dhahran and I knew one of the members who was a dive instructor. So it was that I enrolled in an Open Water training course under the auspices of the Professional Association of Diving Instructors (PADI). Based in the USA, it is a worldwide organisation with branches in many countries.

Open Water is the basic course and there is a great deal of theory taught in the classroom as well as sessions in the comparative safety of the swimming pool. Initially there was no requirement to buy any equipment other than a snorkel, mask and flippers as the instructors in Dhahran had numerous tanks, buoyancy control device, or vest (BCD), regulators, weight belts and sundry other diving paraphernalia. No point in investing sums of money in a hobby which you might end up not liking !

The evening classes went well and the pool sessions were enjoyable, once you overcame the natural anxiety of performing tasks in an unusual location i.e. underwater. The instructors knew their stuff and we learnt all about the complexities of dive tables and the horrors of nitrogen narcosis, or the bends as it is more commonly known. A steady progression was made over the following weeks, from classroom to swimming pool and then finally to my first dive in the sea.

Half Moon Bay was naturally the venue for this first dive and although I had become familiar with the intricacies of regulators, tank pressures and 'O' rings, there was still a sense of nervous excitement as I waded into the sea for the first time.

Perfect clarity made things much easier beneath the waves and the memory of that first gentle descent to the sea bed as the air was slowly released from my BCD, stays with me to this day. My first dive in the shallows of the bay never exceeded a depth of thirty feet. At the conclusion of the dive, it was pronounced a success and I became a fully certified PADI Open Water diver.

At this point a decision had to be made. If I wished to continue diving I would need to acquire my own equipment. The diving opportunities afforded throughout the Gulf and in the region in general, were too spectacular not to take the jump so to speak, so I purchased a brand new regulator, BCD Jacket and two shiny new air tanks. I was all set to go.

Apart from recreational diving, there were further courses available. Having purchased all the equipment, I duly enrolled in the Advanced Diver course in which I discovered that my initial training had barely scratched the surface. This course took place entirely in the sea with a few deeper dives farther out in the Gulf where the depth exceeded seventy feet. There were to be night dives, dives in which you had to completely remove all equipment and swap with your buddy and some deeper dives where a series of mental exercises had to be performed using a waterproof pen and pad.

The Saudi shore slips gently into the warm waters of the Gulf and one could often wade out a considerable distance from the shoreline until the water was at last deep enough to swim. A 'deep dive' in sport diving terms was a depth of sixty feet or more and this therefore required a boat. For the deep dive we journeyed up to Jubail, some fifty miles north where a sleepy fishing village had been transformed into a new industrial city with a deep water port.

The dhow port was located in the original bay around which some older buildings were huddled. It would probably have remained a sleepy fishing port as it had for centuries, prior to the transformation of Saudi Arabia. The obscure fishing village was now being overwhelmed by enormous roads, canals and huge concrete piers which jutted out into the water as far as the eye could see.

Some ten students plus instructors, boarded the dhow which was tied up at the pier. Our destination was an island, an uninhabited coral atoll called Juraid, which lay about twenty five miles north east of Jubail. It was to this tiny speck of sand and coral that the old dhow took us for our deep dive.

It was March and quite a windy day. We didn't think too much of this until we were clear of the bay when the swell became increasingly large. The small dhow bucked and weaved its way through the waves. Although it was eminently seaworthy, it was something of a roller coaster ride and some of our party had begun to feel distinctly unwell long before we reached Juraid.

I have fortunately never suffered from sea sickness, but quite a few of my fellow divers had begun throwing up and many of the others didn't look altogether well. It didn't bode well for the deep dive, however with the small atoll now in sight, the dhow captain brought the boat round to the leeward side where the water was much calmer. He then dropped anchor. With calmer water, the nausea among those who had felt unwell, began to subside and the diving could begin.

The water remained clear despite the turbulence on the surface, though it was incredible to see how rapidly the light diminished during the descent to even thirty feet. At fifty feet and beyond even less sunlight would penetrate beneath the waves and would become a world of darkness. In those days there was still a vibrant and colourful reef surrounding Juraid containing a wealth of fish, crustaceans and anemones. For the first time since I learned to dive, I was able to see the tropical underwater world in all its glory.

A more unusual optional extra on the course was to perform a well dive. Near the local town of Qatif, there were a number of fresh water springs and wells which centuries ago had given rise to this desert oasis and the subsequent settlement. We arrived at one of these wells one Friday morning and prepared to don our equipment. The well was some ninety feet deep and due to the fresh water would be far less buoyant than sea water, especially those in the heavily saline Arabian Gulf just a few miles away.

Less weight was required to submerge in the fresh water and torches, similar to those used in night dives would be required due to the combination of depth and the inability of light to penetrate such a narrow shaft. It was going to be pretty dark at the bottom of a ninety foot well.

The descent was the same as any other, but it got remarkably dark after only five metres and the torches were turned on. The walls of the well appeared to have been scoured by hand, as what appeared to be clean, man-made cuts descended into the depths. Quite how these had been created was a mystery.

From the bottom of the well the distant surface was a pinhole of light. The water was by no means still and a current swirled gently around us, fed by aquifers hundreds of feet below the bottom of the well. Surprisingly, small shrimp like creatures could be seen swimming here and there. We completed some mathematical exercises while kneeling at the bottom and after fifteen minutes we began our slow ascent to the surface, halting for a decompression stop half way up.

I expected to see only blue sky above me as we completed the last part of the ascent, so imagine my shock when suddenly all I could see was the thrashing of horse hooves above me. Not wishing to be on the wrong end of a hoof, we held position about fifteen feet below. After a few minutes the horse thankfully disappeared and we made it to the surface. It turned out that a local had taken his horse for a ride and decided to give it a bath. Only in Arabia!

Over the following months, I participated in a number of dive trips, sometimes returning to Juraid, but also to the smaller atoll of Jana which lay ten miles further out into the Gulf. Sometimes the dives would be at various locations in Half Moon Bay, but with its sandy bottom and shallow water, it lacked the diverse marine life offered by the atolls and was clearly a more suitable venue for sailing and fishing than for scuba diving.

The one exception to this lay around the other side of the bay towards the company town of Abqaiq at a place called Qurrayah. The beach and underwater profile was not unlike the Aramco beach near Dhahran with neither naturally occurring coral reefs, nor a profusion of fish. The enterprising divers of

Abqaiq had however taken matters into their own hands and created an artificial 'reef' composed of pieces of redundant heavy equipment, steel girders, tyres and other bits and pieces of machinery. The 'reef' had been built some ten years earlier and it was now home to a wide variety of aquatic creatures which otherwise would not have been attracted to such an unpromising location.

The next step on the PADI curriculum was the Rescue Diver course. Thinking that this might be fun, I duly enrolled for a course which would include night dives, rescue situations and yet more solving of problems while underwater. I have to say the night dive did make me wonder if it was the sensible thing to do. As part of any diving course you are made acutely aware that the water is a hostile environment and continually reminded of all that can go wrong - especially if you deviate from the original plan. The motto was always 'plan the dive and dive the plan'.

The venue for the night dive was Half Moon Bay with its gently shelving seabed largely devoid of any obstacles. It would not be a deep dive, but would involve for the first time, the use of an underwater compass. It was a moonless night and once beneath the waves it was pitch black and extremely disorienting, not to say a little scary. I was in good hands however as the instructor was very experienced, but nevertheless the motion of the water and complete darkness except for the light from our torches was quite eerie.

I passed the test, but never found night diving a particularly rewarding experience. I would perform only one further night dive some months later over in the Red Sea, but that didn't go entirely to plan.

Chapter 18

Diving The Red Sea

One of the many benefits of working for Aramco in the diving sense at least, was that we could freely use company aircraft to fly across the country to the Red Sea coast at Yanbu which, similar to the town of Jubail on the Gulf coast, had been transformed from a quiet fishing village into an industrial city with a deepwater port. As I mentioned in earlier, T.E. Lawrence had stayed for some time in Yanbu, or Yenbo as it is spelt in his book *The Seven Pillars of Wisdom*. He rested there while taking part in the Arab revolt against the Turks during the First World War, though the old house in which he stayed had long since disappeared.

Aramco had daily flights to Yanbu which took two hours from Dhahran. If seats were available, then employees who were not travelling there for work purposes, could book any spare seats free of charge. Outbound flights from Dhahran to Yanbu were generally fairly empty at the weekends. For a weekend of diving in the spectacular waters of the Red Sea, a Wednesday evening flight was the best option with a Friday afternoon return. Not only could you book a seat, but heavy equipment such as tanks and dive bags with all the other heavy diving paraphernalia were easily accommodated on the company's

Boeing jets which operated on this route.

Air tanks of course could only be carried empty, but this was no problem as they could be filled, also free of charge, at the company's Gas Plant in Yanbu. This would be the first port of call after picking up a hire car from the airport. Accommodation could be found at either the Holiday Inn or the Hyatt, hotels which had both opened during the past couple of years.

Amazingly pristine coral reefs ran virtually the entire length of the Arabian shore from the Gulf of Aqaba in the north, all the way down to Yemen in the south. The reef was punctuated only in two places by the dredging and where explosives had been used at both Jeddah port and more recently in Yanbu, to destroy the reef and allow for the construction of deep water port facilities.

Although the Red Sea is comparatively narrow, it is very deep and unlike the Arabian Gulf, the water stays at a virtually constant temperature all the year round. This has resulted in a proliferation of coral and other marine life unable to tolerate major differences in temperature.

The favoured dive site within relatively easy reach, was about thirty miles north of the burgeoning city out beyond the cement plant. Unattractive though this sounds, it did at least have a kind of road which even non-4WD cars could negotiate. Once the cement plant was out of sight you passed through a small coastguard checkpoint after which you could basically pull up anywhere in order to enter the sea.

Entry into the sea however was not so easy. There were no gently shelving sandy beaches here, instead the shoreline was jagged rocks and coral with wading required through shallows in order to get to the reef drop off. The walk was difficult enough, but made all the more so due to wearing heavy diving gear, flippers and air tanks. Only the wearing of thick rubber dive boots made progress possible over the rocks lying just beneath the surface.

The distance from the shore to the drop-off, which resembled a cliff face, varied from fifty to one hundred feet. In some places there were holes in the rocky floor, sub-aquatic caves, some of which were large enough to descend into and which then allowed the diver to swim out underwater to an opening in the reef face. The first glimpse of the open blue sea when exiting one of these submarine caves was nothing short of phenomenal. I thought that the waters of the Arabian Gulf were clear, but this was on another level altogether. The brilliant colours of the coral and the amazing variety of marine life were truly breathtaking.

Over the following years, I travelled to Yanbu on many occasions with small groups of divers and always enjoyed the exceptional diving conditions. On one occasion as part of a group of four, we decided rather rashly to perform a night dive. The entry as I explained before was not easy even during daylight and after donning our equipment we struggled through the shallow water over the jagged coral rocks towards the drop-off. Buffeted by the surf, some of us fell over while others began to have equipment issues. We were exhausted by the time we reached the drop-off, when we saw a vehicle pull up on the shore next to our cars and shine a powerful spotlight over the water.

We were eventually caught in the beam and there were shouts from the shore. Not knowing who it was, or what the problem might be, we decided to wade back towards the beach where it became apparent that the vehicle and flashlight belonged to the Saudi Coastguard. In broken English they made it clear that they were not keen for us to be out at this hour and that we should only be diving during the day. They did not explain their rationale as we were not breaking any laws as far as we knew.

By now the wind was blowing harder and the surf was becoming rougher. We knew that entering the sea in these conditions would be extremely hazardous, we also knew that it would be best not to ignore the instructions of anyone in uniform. It was almost with a sense of relief that we packed away our equipment and headed back towards town. Perhaps something was telling us that night diving was not a good idea and in fact I never attempted another night dive again.

Chapter 19

Going the Course

Golf was the love of many Americans and it was no surprise to find that in Dhahran as well as some of the other larger Aramco communities, this sport had been catered for in some rudimentary fashion since the early days. Over the decades, the standard of the courses had gradually improved and areas of hitherto barren sand had undergone a remarkable degree of landscaping……they were however still sand.

In the days before the development of huge seawater desalination plants, water was available only through ancient aquifers and was therefore a scarce and valuable commodity. Spraying millions of litres of water on sand to grow grass for a mere sporting activity, was obviously not an option, so a golf course had of necessity to be sand. The grandly titled Rolling Hills Country Club in Dhahran, comprised three nine-hole courses, East, West and South. They were contiguous, so a combination of any two would allow an eighteen hole round of golf.

The fairways consisted of rolled sand, while the 'greens' were in fact brown and used finely grained sand sprayed with crude oil, producing a putting surface not unlike that of finely mown grass. After playing the hole however, the foot and ball marks needed to be raked and rolled, though his was not a job for the golfers.

A worker, usually from the Indian sub-continent, was on hand to perform this task throughout the day and after each group of golfers had completed the hole. He would drag a large rake in concentric circles around the surface until all was ready for the next group of players. Sadly these individuals were not provided with any proper protection from the fierce sun, or other elements during the long day. They would construct rudimentary places of shade among the rocks and bushes, covering themselves where necessary with bits of discarded cardboard boxes, or sheets of metal foil.

The tee boxes were rubber mats with built in tees much like you would see at a golf driving range, but for any shots taken on the fairways, or indeed in the 'rough', players carried a square foot of 'astro turf', or mat as we called it. Local rules therefore permitted the lifting of the ball from its place of rest and onto the astro turf mat from which the next shot would then be played.

The upside of this was that regardless of the actual lie of the ball, fairway or not, the next shot would always be played from a smooth, if artificial, surface. I hadn't played a great deal of golf before arriving in Saudi Arabia, but over the years I got used to playing with a mat. When I ultimately returned to this country I found that hitting the ball on natural grass with its varying lengths, lies and moisture content made golf a great deal more difficult... at least that's my excuse.

The club was a vibrant one with gents and ladies captains, a clubhouse complete with changing rooms and a fast food restaurant. Lines of small golf buggy garages with chargers stood behind the clubhouse and the driving range had canopies over each tee box for shade.

Numerous competitions were held throughout the year. The major ones were the 'Presidents Cup' where prizes were awarded by the Aramco CEO as well as the annual 'Turkey Shoot' which took place just prior to American Thanksgiving Day in November. This was a particular highlight, with every single player guaranteed a large turkey regardless of how appalling their score. I confess that these turkeys were the only prizes I ever won throughout my many years of membership.

In later years, with the widespread availability of desalinated water, many golf courses throughout the Middle East were grassed and equipped with comprehensive sprinkler systems. The Aramco course in Dhahran was no exception and is today a wonderfully green and landscaped area, dotted with palm trees and water hazards. The astro turf mats carried around by golfers over many decades, now but a footnote in history.

Chapter 20

Clouds Gather - The Gulf War

I received a phone call from a close friend one quiet Friday morning on the 2nd August 1990. 'Have you heard what's happened?' he gushed. I hadn't.

He'd been listening to BBC World Service and informed me that overnight, the Iraqi army had invaded the tiny state of Kuwait located just 150 miles to the north. I immediately tuned to the BBC to discover that this event was now the sole topic of world news. Apart from the still sketchy reports, various experts were pronouncing on the geopolitical implications of the situation and what was likely to happen next.

There were constant references to the fact that Iraqi tanks were massing on the Saudi border and this was naturally making everyone in Dhahran a little nervous. Everyone knew of Saddam's reputation as a brutal dictator who had pretty much started the Iran - Iraq war that had dragged on through most of the eighties, but this was completely different. Kuwait was a 'brotherly' Arab country and member of the Gulf Cooperation Council (GCC) which was effectively a miniature version of NATO. An attack upon one state was considered an attack upon all and the other members were obliged to come to its aid.

As you can imagine, this made for many interesting

conversations the following day at work. Everyone had their own opinion of what might happen next. It was interesting that for the first 48 hours, the local Arab media remained silent. It was as if nothing had happened. Fortunately, access to foreign radio broadcasts meant that we were 'in the loop' so to speak and even though the governments of Saudi Arabia and others were maintaining an official silence, we knew, or at least thought we knew, exactly what was happening.

It didn't take a military genius to work out that Iraq's army overwhelmingly outnumbered the military capabilities of both Saudi Arabia and those of the other GCC nations. More importantly, the richest prize of all, the Saudi oilfields, not to mention myself, was now an easy three hour drive for Saddam's massed tank columns.

Of equal concern, was the information being broadcast regarding Iraq's alleged stockpiles of chemical, or biological weapons. They had used chemical weapons before, both against the Kurds and the Iranians. Who was to say that they would not use them again?

Familiarity with a place is a strange thing. By late summer of 1990, I had been living in Saudi Arabia for more than eleven years and for the most part I felt it to be an entirely safe environment and one in which I felt very much at ease. The thought that we might at any time be invaded by Iraqi hordes may have been worrying on one level, but on another, familiarity with the place somehow made it seem not quite so threatening. We went to work as usual, played golf in the late afternoon and pretty much continued our lives as normal. Everything seemed outwardly normal, but we did start to pay more attention to the international news broadcasts.

In the near absence of any firm news from either the company, or Saudi government, the expat grapevine surged into overdrive. The consensus seemed to be that if Saddam had intended to invade the Eastern Province, then his tanks would already have rolled into Dhahran. Nevertheless, it seemed prudent to take a few precautions just in case we were wrong. There was quite a queue at the company gas station that evening as like-minded individuals filled up the tanks of their cars and trucks, plus any jerry cans or other containers they might possess.

Suspecting that the airports would be closed in the event of an invasion, the basic plan was to drive in the opposite direction, either across the Arabian peninsula to Riyadh and then perhaps onto Jeddah, or south towards either Qatar, or Abu Dhabi in the United Arab Emirates. All of these options would likely be beyond the logistical range and capabilities of the Iraqis.

It was at least a plan and so I topped up my car to the brim with fuel and filled some large plastic containers with water which would be kept in the boot of my car ready to evacuate at a moment's notice. Meanwhile, ears were kept glued to the radio broadcasts for the latest updates.

Within days of the invasion, the crisis had escalated to the UN Security Council and it seemed that Saddam had perhaps bitten off a little more than he had bargained for. The United States in particular, in the shape of President Bush was particularly strident in his condemnation of the Iraqi invasion. This possibly gave Saddam pause for thought and over the next few days it seemed that the possibility of Iraq advancing any further south had receded.

Chapter 21

Gathering Storm - The Gulf War

Dhahran is situated on a low hill a couple of miles west of Dhahran airport which is an enormous military airbase and at that time, also a commercial airport. Within hours of President Bush announcing 'Operation Desert Shield' a continuous stream of enormous US Air Force transport planes began landing at the airport, depositing men, supplies and weapons.

It was a round the clock operation and if anyone ever needed reminding of the United States' enormous military capacity, one only had to look at the vast scale of this operation as it unfolded before our very eyes. The future was still very much uncertain, but we all slept a little easier knowing that the US Cavalry had arrived.

A couple of days later, I was sitting in my office when an American soldier, a captain wearing full combat gear knocked on my door. He was searching for detailed maps of the area and had been advised that the Technical Library located within the Engineering Organisation might be a good place to try. He had come to the wrong floor, but I took him up one floor and wishing him luck, introduced him to the supervisor of the technical library.

Word soon spread that spearhead soldiers who had flown in

on some of the early flights were bivouacked in foxholes close by with very little in the way of creature comforts. It was still the ferocious heat of summer and it could not have been a pleasant environment.

At the instigation of a number of American employees, many of whom were former servicemen, an informal network was quickly set up whereby employees would collect small groups of soldiers from their nearby camps and bring them into Dhahran. They could then have a shower, have their uniforms washed, make a telephone call home and possibly sample the delights of some 'home brew'.

That first week, I picked up three soldiers from the US 24th Mechanised Infantry, an elite spearhead division who had hitherto been based in Fort Stewart, Georgia. They all seemed to be giants, standing at least six feet four inches tall. They were very grateful for the opportunity to indulge in a few creature comforts as they had literally been sleeping in a tent since their arrival, existing entirely on MRE's (Meals Ready to Eat). These were small, brown plastic bags of de-hydrated food ready to eat once they had been boiled in water for ten minutes. Not very appetising perhaps, but it enabled them to survive.

As you can imagine, they were extremely pleased to come in out of the hot desert, even if only for a few hours. In the early days of Desert Shield the spearhead troops didn't have an awful lot of creature comforts, but over the coming weeks, as the airlift continued around the clock, more equipment and support arrived. They gradually began to move out from the perimeter they had placed around Dhahran and the other major oil facilities and into more forward positions.

Once we had started this voluntary hospitality system, it

continued throughout the operation until the end of the war the following February. When British soldiers arrived a month or so later, the system was expanded to include them. By this time it was less of a necessity, but the soldiers nevertheless enjoyed some time off from their normal duties at their various desert camps.

The Ramada-Dhahran Palace Hotel was located just a short distance outside one of the main gates into Dhahran. The car park at the front of the hotel was the appointed rendezvous point for two busloads of British soldiers. As one of the coordinators of the scheme, I had organised about twenty colleagues to come to the hotel car park where each would collect three or four soldiers to take them back to their respective houses. In order to avoid any terrorist attacks, the British Army had decided that soldiers on these trips would not be in uniform, although some of them would be armed.

I arrived there a little ahead of time and was pacing idly around the car park in the late afternoon sun. An army Land-Rover eventually pulled in and two female soldiers wearing combat fatigues and carrying very large rifles got out. They informed me that the buses would be arriving within ten minutes and that they had been sent on ahead to 'secure the area'.

A few minutes later after checking the perimeter of the car park they suddenly dropped to the ground, assuming prone positions on the tarmac while checking and re-checking the mechanisms on their guns. I was just left standing in the middle of the car park wondering if they knew something that I didn't.

I'm pleased to say that whatever they may have been expecting, didn't happen and the buses arrived without incident.

My colleagues turned up in their cars to ferry them back to their homes in small groups. The hosting of soldiers, both American and British went on throughout the remainder of the year. Liaising with senior officers of both the United States and British military, company employees enabled thousands of soldiers, airman and sailors to visit the camp during this time.

Groups of employees would take it in turns to co-host larger groups of soldiers at weekends as this was sometimes easier to coordinate. It was a good feeling to show our appreciation to the men and women who were putting their lives on the line to protect us and that we could give them a welcome respite from life under canvas in a hot desert camp.

I certainly met some interesting young men and women who had a few stories to tell. I remember one evening hosting a group of four young soldiers from the Royal Scots Dragoon Guards. They were hard, young men from Glasgow with very broad accents. One of them - Sean, told me that he had left the army some six months earlier, having got bored with the routine of peacetime army life in Germany. When the possibility of some real action arose, he had immediately re-enlisted.

He wanted, as he put it; 'to rip the heads off some Iraqis.' I was reminded of the famous words of the Duke of Wellington who, upon completing a review of his troops uttered the immortal line; 'I don't know what they do to the enemy, but by God they frighten me.'

One Friday afternoon I was invited to the house of an American friend, a former marine, for a barbecue. On arrival, I found a contingent of about fifteen US Marines, from the same platoon and amazingly discovered that they were all full-blooded Cherokee Indians. They were inevitably called Brad and Chuck etc. but they also had Cherokee names. I had never knowingly met any American Indians before, so it was fascinating to hear their stories.

The Saudi government, which had initially acted like a rabbit caught in car headlights, belatedly acknowledged there was a situation and told its citizens that it unreservedly condemned the actions of Iraq. It went on to say that it had asked the United States and other friendly nations to help them drive out the aggressor from the brotherly land of Kuwait. The Kuwaiti government i.e. the Al Sabah family were now living in Riyadh having hastily decamped from Kuwait as soon as they got wind of Iraqi tanks rumbling across the border.

The extent to which this was a popular move among the locals was difficult to gauge. Clearly the Al Saud were no friends of Saddam, but they were torn over inviting the military forces of non-believers to enter the holy land of Islam to potentially fight against their fellow Muslims. There was consequently no overt welcome from the locals for the foreign troops arriving on their soil. There was however an acceptance in most quarters, that it was a situation only foreign forces could address. It was unfortunate, but nevertheless a necessity.

Some conservative elements held a different view and would in time, lead to the many conflicts and some of the fundamentalist violence we see today. One of the major gripes incredibly, was that American and British women soldiers were driving military vehicles in a country that would not even allow its own women to drive any kind of vehicle. This, coupled with the fact that foreign infidels including women, were protecting Saudi men was too great an affront to their honour for some to bear. Most expats were quite enjoying their discomfiture.

There were numerous opportunities for locals to make a great deal of money from this crisis and many of them grabbed it with both hands. Owners of land, construction equipment, vehicles, water wells and a host of other services made an enormous amount of money by providing the ever-growing armed forces with their almost insatiable demands. The Saudi government were bankrolling the entire military operation, so it could be argued that this was just economic re-cycling.

As the military forces continued to build, we followed every diplomatic twist and turn being played out at the United Nations and in various capitals around the world. It seemed that Iraq had few friends and sadly for them, their leader seemed to have little concept of how badly his strategy was playing out to the wider world. The taking of human hostages in the early weeks after the invasion, was a similar miscalculation and succeeded only in turning him into a bigger international pariah than he already was.

Meanwhile life in Dhahran settled back into a more normal pace now that the threat of an imminent Iraqi invasion had begun to fade. Clearly no-one but a madman would even contemplate invading Saudi Arabia now, but then, Saddam was clearly a madman.

Surprisingly, there hadn't been the mass exodus of expatriates which would have been understandable, during this time. Many of us who had been there for some considerable time didn't feel particularly vulnerable and perhaps in some respects the situation had injected a frisson of excitement into our otherwise routine lives. When Kuwait was invaded in early August, many wives and children of expatriates were already back at home for the summer. Most elected to stay there until the situation was resolved, while the men continued working.

By the end of October, the British Embassy had arranged for all British passport holders to be issued with gas masks. Termed NBC masks (Nuclear, Biological Chemical) these were all brand new. The US consulate had already issued masks to American citizens, but by comparison these looked pretty old and well worn. For once the 'Brits' had an advantage over the Americans.

Gradually, we employees began to notice certain changes. In a seemingly anxious bid to retain its labour force, the company started to relax certain long-held policies. One example was the issuing of multiple exit/re-entry visas and allowing senior staff to hold their own passports.

It had long been the practice of the Saudi Government that most foreign workers had to have an initial entry visa to arrive in Saudi Arabia and were then required to obtain an exit/re-entry visa in order to travel outside the country. This meant that passports were kept by the individual's employer who would obtain the visas - subject to completing the necessary paperwork with the appropriate signatures. It effectively meant that you were a hostage of sorts.

Some complained about this procedure, but I viewed it as one of a number of personal restrictions to which you had to submit in order to live and work in the country, it's just the way it was. There would be no point in holding your own passport when you did not have the necessary visa to leave. On the whole the system worked well although there was always a hint of nervousness when you visited the passport office prior to departing on vacation - had they in fact got the visa? ... had they perhaps lost your passport? You did hear of some horror stories, but fortunately this never happened to me.

It was during the run up to the Gulf War that this 'rule' which had been in place for decades, miraculously changed overnight - at least for westerners. Quite what drove this change was hard to pin down. Some speculated that they desperately needed to avoid a mass exodus of expatriates - effectively shutting down oil production. Some thought that pressure had been applied to the Saudi government by the US and other allies to end this 'feudal' system. Whatever the reason, it was particularly welcome in this time of uncertainty. We now had multiple exit/re-entry visas stamped in our passports and kept them securely at home.

Nearby Bahrain, a mere one-hour drive across the recently completed causeway, was now accessible at a moment's notice without having to go through the laborious and long-winded procedure of having to apply for a one-time exit/re-entry visa. My friends and I therefore began to visit Bahrain on a far more regular basis, if only to get out of Dhahran and have a civilised drink in a hotel. Of course Bahrain was just as much in the potential firing line as Dhahran and its airport too was hosting huge numbers of military aircraft from the many countries involved in the US led coalition.

It was just the sense of normality of having a meal in a nice restaurant and visiting the many bars available throughout Manama the capital city. We took our NBC masks as a precaution and sure enough the first night we were there, the air raid sirens sounded at dusk. We later discovered that spy satellites could detect the launch of a scud missile, but could not know the specific target. Air raid sirens would therefore sound as a precautionary measure in Bahrain, Dhahran, Riyadh and Tel Aviv, the most likely targets.

We were now also able to access satellite news channels on television, primarily CNN, but also the American Armed Forces Radio and Television Service (AFRTS) for the first time. The company even implemented a 'loyalty bonus' a monthly increment of fifteen percent which would be paid over and above our regular salaries.

Dhahran airport was still a hive of activity with transport planes continuing to land around the clock. As a fighter base there were also constant sorties of Royal Saudi Air Force, US Air Force and RAF planes overhead. It seemed that all military hardware which existed throughout the world had been relocated to the Eastern Province of Saudi Arabia.

As the debate in the UN Security Council hotted up, it became clear that Iraq would either have to withdraw from Kuwait, or would be physically removed. Anyone who knew anything about the Arab mentality would have known from the outset that Saddam would never do the sensible thing and back down. This would have been an unacceptable loss of face and anything, even the loss of thousands of his own troops would be preferable to that.

Thus the scene was slowly being set, Saddam had painted himself into a corner and he wasn't likely to be withdrawing anytime soon. Resolutions condemning the Iraqi invasion were duly passed in the Security Council and finally a deadline date was set for the complete withdrawal of Iraqi forces from Kuwait by 15th January, 1991.

There was still plenty of time for further military build-up and the addition of other national forces to the international coalition that had been assembled. It looked increasingly likely that this was going to be the first time the United States had gone to war since the military and political disaster of Vietnam. There were understandably a lot of nerves and true to form, the world's media played its part by constantly talking up the size and capability of the Iraqi military machine as well as their possible, or even likely use of chemical and biological weapons.

Dhahran airport perimeter was now ringed with a series of defensive measures, including serried ranks of Patriot missiles, which were lined up along the airbase perimeter just half a mile away from my house in Dhahran Hills. The British Consulate had long had a system of wardens who were the conduits along which official messages could be disseminated among the British population resident in Saudi Arabia.

As can be imagined, this system had been working overtime during this period and it was through this conduit that we were advised that a presentation would be taking place at a hotel in Al Khobar in which an RAF ballistic missile expert would give an assessment of Iraq's missile capabilities.

This was naturally the hottest ticket in town that night. In the presentation, we were basically told that the type of ballistic missiles available to the Iraqi military were the fairly obsolete Russian 'Scud' type which had a range of approximately 300 miles. We were well within range of that, but he stated that at the maximum extent of their range, they were wildly inaccurate and the chances of being hit by one were negligible, but more of that later.

With regard to warheads it was considered that these were likely to be conventional explosive types, but the possibility of Iraq having weaponised either a chemical or biological warhead could not be entirely discounted. We were therefore given advice on how to set up what were euphemistically called 'safe rooms' in our homes. This would essentially be a room with no windows and which could be internally sealed with duct tape around the door.

For some reason which I haven't quite been able to work out, it seems that we are inclined to prefer being blown to pieces by explosives than poisoned by gas or biological weapons. At any rate we left the presentation feeling a lot more relaxed about our situation in the event that hostilities commenced. We continued with our hosting of soldiers and on some occasions were able to visit some of their positions out in the desert towards the Kuwaiti border.

Once the UN resolution had been passed the countdown began, but first there was Christmas and I was due a leave. Looking back, it's strange that I decided to return to the UK for two weeks without a second thought about not returning to a potential war zone, even though the rest of the world seemed to be hanging on tenterhooks. I had a relaxing break at home before boarding a flight back to Dhahran where the airport was still functioning as a commercial airport, although it had to be said that most airlines had cancelled their services at this point.

The days were counting down and it seemed as though the allies had everything ready. It was now a question of waiting until the deadline for an Iraqi withdrawal in accordance with the Security Council resolution. Any remaining expatriate wives and children took the last planes out as air services from Dhahran and other parts of the Gulf would shortly be suspended.

Some Saudi employees gradually began to disappear from

work around this time, due to sudden mysterious illnesses of family members who just happened to live in Jeddah. Despite the bonus system in operation, the pressure began to mount and some expat employees also decided to depart at this time, many of whom were undoubtedly under pressure from their wives.

It was interesting to see the way that different people handled this pressure. Many individuals whom you felt would be able to take the situation in their stride and remain in place, were often the first to leave and those perhaps that you thought might crack, turned out to display a hitherto hidden degree of stoicism. After the last flight left in January it was too late to change your mind.

I had always adopted a fairly fatalistic, though optimistic view on the situation and I did not feel that it was particularly dangerous to stay. How wrong I was!

Chapter 22

The Storm Breaks - The Gulf War

In the early hours of 16th January 1991, the air was filled with the roar of jet fighters a few hundred feet above me. The roar continued throughout the night and made further sleep impossible. My house lay more or less directly under the flight path as wave after wave of fully-armed jet fighters took off from the runway just half a mile away.

As sure as night follows day, two hours later, the air raid sirens sounded above the noise of the jets and as I was already fully awake, I got out of bed, entered my 'safe room' and donned the NBC mask. I put adhesive masking tape to create a seal between the door and door frame in accordance with the previously issued instructions. I had neglected to put a chair into the bathroom and so pulled myself onto the marble bathroom surface along from the sink.

I sat there for possibly an hour, listening intently for sounds of explosions while studying myself in the full length mirror on the opposite wall. The black mask was heavy and becoming more uncomfortable by the minute. The canister containing the filter element, which was screwed into the side of the mouthpiece, looked like some horrific rubberised carbuncle.

It was my habit to sleep with no clothes on and as I surveyed myself in the mirror, naked except for the huge rubber mask, I realised that it wasn't a good look.

Tired and uncomfortable, it was at that point I decided to take it off and get back into bed. I concluded that if anything happened, at least I would not cut quite such a ridiculous figure if I was pulled from the rubble.

As the air campaign gathered speed, the jet sorties flying overhead were more frequent and from my back garden I would see them passing overhead just after take-off, laden with bombs and missiles. There were F-15s of the USAF and Royal Saudi Air Force as well as RAF Tornadoes and they would scream overhead around the clock en route to attack the Iraqi forces. The air war would continue non-stop for forty-two days and the air raid sirens we had first heard on the opening night of the air campaign, became a regular feature of our lives.

Typically the sirens would sound at dusk, a sure sign that the allied reconnaissance aircraft had detected movement of Saddam's mobile Scud launchers which had usually been parked up under bridges, or otherwise hidden in order to avoid detection during the day. The sirens were triggered by the firing of a missile and would therefore go off regardless of the direction of the missile. It could have been directed towards Riyadh, Bahrain, or Tel Aviv for all we knew.

Most of us had been taking our gas masks into the office as a precaution and we generally kept them within reach at all times. It was not long before the first scud winged its way in our direction. The loudest bang I had ever heard happened one evening when I was sitting in my lounge watching TV. The bang and shockwave was so great that pictures fell off my walls and the large sliding glass door out to the patio bowed inwards.

I threw myself on the floor expecting at any moment to be showered in breaking glass and masonry, but thankfully the glass door held firm and the house didn't collapse on my head.

The noise I had heard had not been the explosion of an incoming Scud missile, but the noise of a Patriot missile being fired to intercept it. The missile launchers had been positioned along the airport perimeter with one such battery positioned a mere quarter of a mile from my house. I learned later that these missiles break the sound barrier even as they leave their launchers. The noise and sound I had heard was not the sound of an explosion, but was in fact a sonic boom. It would not be too long before I witnessed a launch.

The start of Rolling Hills Road as it left main camp near the Golf Clubhouse was the highest spot in Dhahran, the land to the south and east sloping gently away towards the sea. Before reaching the sea, the sprawling airbase and its runways were clear to see. It was at this point in the fading light of dusk as I was driving back to my house in Dhahran Hills, when I heard the sound of five rapid explosions.

On the airport perimeter, I saw an incredible salvo of five patriots being launched simultaneously from their pods. Two of the missiles shot straight upwards while two others made amazingly sharp right and left turns only a hundred feet above the ground. They then streaked off in different directions, gradually gaining altitude as they disappeared into the sky. I stopped the car and pulled to the side of the road. This may not have been the smartest driving manoeuvre I have ever made, for I realised that the fifth missile of the multiple launch was headed straight in my direction and it was worryingly low.

I instinctively ducked as it streaked over my car no more than a hundred feet above me before heading skyward on a vertical trajectory. A few seconds later above the thin cloud layer, there was a flash and a muffled explosion.

I was aware that the patriots were armed with proximity fuses which detonated when closing on an incoming missile. The intent is to explode the warhead, but failing that, to at least knock the incoming scud off its intended trajectory. This meant that the scud could come down anywhere, but the warhead would remain live and would still explode upon hitting the ground.

I concluded that I was parked in what might well be the point of impact, so I drove off in some haste, at least I would be a moving target. Fortunately there was no major impact within the Dhahran area so I assume the incoming missile warhead had been destroyed. The Rolling Hills Country Club where I had witnessed this extraordinary aerial duel was however liberally showered with pieces of hot and twisted metal which were collected over the next few days by camp residents for souvenirs. I have one in my desk drawer to this day.

The air war proceeded for forty two days. Days of relentless sorties day and night. It was wearing. Finally the ground invasion of Kuwait began, but the Iraqis were still able to launch a few defiant scud missile attacks. It was the last day of the conflict when a scud was launched in the direction of Dhahran, whether it was taken down by a patriot, or whether it continued to its planned destination is not known, but it landed in the nearby city of Al Khobar about a mile from the airport. Not only did it land in the city, but right on top of a building which was being used by US troops, killing all twenty eight military personnel inside.

In truth we had become a bit blasé over the preceding weeks. The air raid sirens warning of any incoming scuds had either been knocked down by patriots, or landed harmlessly somewhere in the desert. There had mercifully been no chemical, biological or nuclear warheads, but this last attack was a reminder that conventional warheads were extremely deadly. If this had happened in the early days of the war, I suspect that there would have been a mass exodus of the population of the Eastern Province.

The ground war was over almost as soon as it had begun. The relentless air campaign and the overwhelming superiority of the ground forces soon prevailed over what was left of the Iraqi army and victory was duly declared. The air raid sirens fell silent and we were able to put our NBC masks back in the wardrobe, peel the sticky tape from the 'safe-room' door and generally return to some kind of normality.

Although many foreign troops were to remain in Kuwait and indeed Saudi Arabia for quite some time, the vast majority of troops and equipment were gradually shipped back to their countries of origin. So much had been brought into the country during the six months since August, that shipping it back again would take almost as long.

I recall driving down the corniche road south of Al Khobar one afternoon past a line of US tanks, self-propelled guns and armoured vehicles which stretched for about five miles, all waiting for transport ships at Dammam and Jubail ports. In between some of the American vehicles were a few captured Iraqi tanks - Russian T-72s which I recall had been vaunted by some 'experts' during the cold war as being a match for anything we had in the west. All I can say is that in the light of the Arabian sun, they looked decidedly puny against the much larger American ones parked besides them.

In retreating from Kuwait, the Iraqis brought a new and literal meaning to the age old strategy of 'scorched earth'. They set fire to every oil well in Kuwait before they left. The resulting environmental and economic impact was enormous. For months after the liberation, we would wake up to smoky skies until the numerous well fires were finally extinguished. It was not only the fires which caused the damage, the valves on many of the pipelines which fed the oil terminal at Ahmadi on the Kuwaiti coast had been deliberately destroyed, spilling vast quantities of crude oil into the blue waters of the Gulf. It was an horrific act of international vandalism.

For years afterwards a visit to the formerly pristine beach at Najmah near Ras Tanura would mean picking your way around globules of oil scattered across the white sand. This was a hundred miles south of Kuwait, so heaven knows what conditions must have been like further north. Nature however has an amazing capacity to deal with such calamities and whatever the possible unseen consequences of this action, when I visited the beach a year later, there was no trace of the oil.

The families of employees who had departed prior to the war began to return, though sadly some of them never did. Some of those employees who had decided to leave before things got too hot also returned. Those of us who stayed throughout the conflict were rewarded with an extra months pay or 'loyalty bonus' as the Company called it. It was most appreciated, but things somehow never quite seemed the same after the war.

Although the Saudi government made a big thing of the international coalition restoring the Amir of Kuwait to his rightful position, there were many Saudis who were more ambivalent about the whole thing. The fact that foreign troops had planted their boots onto the holy sand of Arabia and furthermore used a great many women troops to defend the country still rankled with many.

No-one gave too much thought to this sentiment at the time, but over the next decade, it would gradually fester and rumble throughout the Middle East, creating ripples which would be felt around the world and have long lasting repercussions which exist to this day.

Chapter 23

Time for a Change

My daughter was born in August 1988. Although I was still on bachelor status, the company permitted frequent visits by close family members and would obtain the necessary visitor visas. The costs of flights etc. were for the employee's account. My wife and subsequently my wife and daughter, had utilised this facility extensively ever since 1982. I was entitled to three paid vacations per year and as they typically visited me twice per calendar year, it meant that we could be together for eight months out of twelve.

By 1992 my daughter, aged four was due to start school in the UK that September. I had been offered a married status contract on a number of occasions which, had I accepted, meant they could have lived with me permanently. My daughter's formal education would have started in either in the Aramco American school in Dhahran, or at the British Academy in Al Khobar.

There were many family discussions, but I finally concluded that as easy as life was, after fifteen years I had been there long enough. My daughter started school in the UK in late 1992 and they paid their final visit to Saudi Arabia the following year after which I handed in my notice. I would be leaving at the end of 1993.

Leaving was more difficult than I had imagined and there would be many farewell parties and celebrations. Sadly, I would be leaving behind many good friends that I had made over the past fifteen years. Andy, the ginger-haired man, now turned grey, had picked me up from the airport when I arrived as a young twenty six year old and had become a close friend over the past fifteen years. He insisted on taking me back to the airport for my final departure, saying; 'I picked you up and I'll take you back.'

My wife was fully involved in her family business which we had co-purchased with her father and brother about six years earlier. We were financially comfortable and I wasn't really interested in looking to resume a career in England. I therefore decided to do something I had always wanted to do which was to write. Working from home, I was able to take my daughter to and from school.

I have to confess that it took me quite a while to settle down, but I eventually got into a routine and became used to the English weather. I gradually began to build a social life, though I never lost touch with the close friends I made in Saudi Arabia.

As a family we continued to travel the world and life was good. I threw myself into writing. I wrote articles on a variety of topics, many of which were published in various magazines and journals and completed three novels which all failed to find a publisher.

There is an old saying in the writing community that goes along the lines of 'if you can't entirely wallpaper your house with publisher and agent rejection slips, then you haven't really been trying'. It's an interesting statement, but I found the steady fall of rejection letters on the doormat, ultimately dispiriting.

Chapter 24

A Second Coming

I had no thoughts of returning to the Middle East. My wife's business was successful and my daughter was progressing well at school, but after ten years, I was looking for a new challenge... but what?

Quite by coincidence, one day early in 2004 I received an e-mail from a former colleague in Aramco. She was a Saudi lady whose husband worked for a small engineering design company in Al Khobar, dealing almost exclusively with my former employer. They were expanding their business and looking for someone to run their contracts and human resources department and did I know of anyone who might be suitable, or whether I might be interested.

I don't think I replied at the time, after all it had been eleven years since I had left the desert kingdom and although there had been good times, it was pretty much a closed chapter as far as I was concerned. I had built a life back home with many friends and acquaintances.

The idea must have remained somewhere locked in my head. About six months later, something possessed me to make contact with my former colleague to ask whether the position had been filled. She replied by return and said that it had not.

I was at something of a loose end at the time. My daughter had turned sixteen and didn't require, or want as much supervision as previously. Perhaps it might an idea to dip my toes back into the desert sands once again. Oil prices were buoyant and this inevitably meant that there would be a great deal of economic activity in that part of the world.

Before making any rash decisions, I decided to do some research. Might my former employer, Aramco also be hiring? Could there be interesting opportunities in some of the other Gulf states, Bahrain, Qatar, Oman or the United Arab Emirates? I decided to fly out, not only to meet the owner of the engineering company who had initially contacted me, but also to visit Qatar, Abu Dhabi and Dubai.

The meeting with the owner of the company was at a hotel in Bahrain. It went very well and the job was duly offered. I told him that I would think about it, but first wanted to look at other opportunities in the Gulf. I flew around the Gulf states for a week, but sometimes you just go with what you know. I knew Saudi Arabia very well and I therefore accepted the job.

My only reservations were about living in a compound in Al Khobar or Dammam. Some of these compounds were very well appointed, but I had been thoroughly spoiled during the fifteen years spent living in Dhahran - more akin to a small Midwest town in the United States than a desert outpost. I couldn't imagine living within the narrow confines of a small compound with daily prayer calls from nearby mosques arousing me from my slumbers at five every morning. I therefore stipulated in my acceptance, that I intended to live in Bahrain and commute daily into Saudi Arabia, something a growing number of expatriates were doing.

I flew back to the UK and prepared for my second departure to the desert. This time, just like the last, I told myself that it would only be for a year or two. In the intervening months between the job being offered and actually arriving, I had contacted a number of friends with whom I had remained in touch for the past eleven years and discovered that many of my former acquaintances and colleagues were still out there. I would have a ready-made social circle.

I flew back to a changed Saudi Arabia. The old airport in Dhahran had been replaced by a huge, new airport built in the desert west of Dammam. The cities were larger, the roads were busier. These were just the physical changes, but there were other, less obvious ones. The events of 9/11, the invasion of Afghanistan and the second gulf war had given rise to Islamic terrorist activities within the kingdom and beyond.

There had been a number of incidents in the Eastern Province during the past ten years. The blowing up of a US military facility in 1996 and the more recent murders of some expatriates in Al Khobar, signs that this was not the altogether peaceful place I remembered.

The company offices were in the centre of Al Khobar and I was temporarily housed in a small compound a couple of miles away. The first week was spent meeting all the staff which numbered around two hundred and fifty. There was also the necessity of being assigned a company car, obtaining a Residents Visa, a Saudi Drivers Licence and crucially having a multiple exit-re-entry visa stamped in my passport. This process took a couple of weeks.

As I would be dealing frequently with my former employer - Saudi Aramco, I had to obtain an Aramco Contractor ID. This necessitated attending the Aramco ID unit housed in a building outside the main camp area. I went with my Government Affairs representative and after completing the photograph and fingerprinting procedure, waited patiently with many others for the card to be issued. In my case this seemed to be taking an inordinate length of time.

Eventually one of the Aramco security employees came over to speak to me. 'You already have a card.' he announced. I was mystified for a moment and then the penny dropped. Of course I had once had a card….eleven years ago ! I explained that I had been an Aramco employee and that my card had been returned when I departed back in 1993. He seemed satisfied with my answer and went away. I was impressed that the Industrial Security system had picked up my name and fingerprint records from eleven years earlier.

When I had all the necessary paperwork, I went over to Bahrain to look for some suitable accommodation. I got in touch with an agency which rented out apartments and villas to expatriates and met one of their representatives. Bahrain is a very small island nation of only three hundred square miles, stretching only fifty kilometres from north to south and a mere fifteen kilometres from east to west. The southern two thirds of the island is largely unpopulated desert with all the urban areas situated in the north and centred around the capital, Manama. The country has a total population of a little over one-million, half of whom are non-Bahrainis.

My requirements in looking for an apartment were that it should be in the Manama area and crucially, with a reasonably short drive to the Saudi causeway. I found the perfect location in the Seef district on the northern coast, a mere ten minute drive from the centre of Manama and only a fifteen minute drive to the causeway.

It was in a small block of furnished apartments right next door to one of the tallest buildings in Bahrain - the Almoayyed Tower sheathed in reflective blue glass and just across the road from what was at that time the largest shopping centre on the island, the Seef Mall.

Boasting a gym and a small indoor swimming pool, the apartment had three large bedrooms and a lounge area with a sea view. A monthly rent was agreed and I was ready to move in the following weekend.

So my new life in the Middle East began....once again! In some respects it was a kind of homecoming, because this strange and alien land really did feel like home. Mindful of the possibility of terrorist attacks however, something I had never had to think about before, I began to take simple precautions such as varying my route into the office and avoiding certain locations.

Chapter 25

Island Life

I soon found out that I wasn't the only person who had arrived in Bahrain at that time. My unexpected fellow resident, on a temporary basis at least, was none other than the recently acquitted Michael Jackson who had escaped to the comparative anonymity of Bahrain to get away from an intrusive media. One thing that could be said about Bahrain was that it was a great respecter of privacy and like most of the Gulf countries, took a very dim view of anything other than government authorised journalism.

I had calculated the drive from the apartment to the causeway entrance, on the highway which passed close to my apartment, would take me fifteen minutes. At the toll booths I would then pay the one-way toll of two Bahraini Dinars, the equivalent of three pounds. This allowed you to drive to the artificial island in the middle of the causeway, the effective border between the two countries and housing all the passport and customs checkpoints. The process went as follows;

Firstly, pick up a receipt for causeway fee at causeway entrance and drive to the centre

Secondly, hand your passport to the Bahrain passport control for exit stamp out.

Thirdly, drive across the 'border' to the Saudi passport control for the stamp in.

Finally, drive to Saudi customs for possible car and personal inspection.

The journey could then continue on to Saudi Arabia.

The speed of this process was dependent upon three things; firstly the volume of traffic, secondly the number of lanes open for both passport and customs check and thirdly and most crucially, the speed at which the various passport and customs personnel felt like performing their jobs.

I had calculated that if the causeway was not busy, then the overall journey from home to office in the morning would take an average of one hour. The causeway was usually quiet in the morning and so an hour was the norm. Occasionally it could take a little longer for a variety of the reasons mentioned earlier, or heavy traffic on the Saudi side. Office hours were seven in the morning until five in the evening and it was a five day week. I would therefore set my alarm for five thirty and usually make it to the office on time.

The journey home was a different matter, the causeway was always busier in the evenings and the closer it got to the weekends, or national holidays, it became even busier. Although Bahrain had some oil revenues from an offshore oilfield it shared with Saudi Arabia, much of its economy was based upon the leisure and entertainment industry. This catered for both expatriates and Saudis who were denied any form of public entertainment in Saudi Arabia. Weekends always meant a heavy volume of traffic heading towards Bahrain from the Eastern Province of Saudi Arabia and beyond.

With the weekend falling on Thursday and Friday,

Wednesday evenings could be a nightmare with tailbacks extending two or three miles back towards the Saudi end of the causeway. Always eager to get away on time on Wednesdays, my heart would sink some evenings as I saw the length of the queue. It wasn't just the long line of traffic however, it was the fact that orderly queuing was an alien concept to the Arabs. The jostling and jockeying for position from the two lanes on the bridge, to the point where the road widened into the multiple passport control lanes, produced a free-for-all that had to be seen to be believed.

Sometimes all the booths would be manned and functioning and sometimes they would not. Often the booth dealing with a particular line of traffic would suddenly close even though there was a long line of vehicles waiting. This would trigger a feverish rush of drivers attempting to squeeze into the next nearest line with much honking of horns and gesticulation. Sometimes the red light on a hitherto idle booth would suddenly turn green indicating that it was now manned, leading to a Le Mans style sprint to get to the head of that queue. Vehicle collisions were not uncommon, which led to further confusion and delay.

It was in short, chaos and I sometimes doubted the wisdom of my decision to live in Bahrain. The longest time it took me to get home was four and a half hours one Wednesday evening prior to a long weekend, although this, I'm glad to say, was exceptional. My typical journey home would usually take around two hours. Leaving work at five meant that I wouldn't get back to my apartment until seven, tired and hungry. Exercise had been a big part of my daily routine for many years, yet now it would be confined to the weekend.

I gradually got used to my daily international commute and

notwithstanding the often frequent delays on the causeway, felt that I had made the right decision to live in Bahrain. I was in the peculiar position of having official residency in Saudi Arabia, yet living in Bahrain where I had no official residency permit. The Bahraini government were fairly relaxed about this situation and it didn't prevent me from renting an apartment, or indeed much else. As far as the authorities were concerned, I left the country every day except at the weekends.

The biggest social circles for most British expatriates were the four clubs - The British Club, The Rugby Club, The Yacht Club and The Dilmun Club. The British Club was the most venerable, established in 1935 as stated proudly above the arched, white stucco entrance. In those days Bahrain was a British Protectorate, only becoming fully independent in 1971.

The club was located in the Adliya district, a fairly central area of Manama. It boasted two excellent restaurants, three bars, a theatre, large outdoor swimming pool and two tennis courts. Like all of the clubs, entry was restricted to members and their guests, although there was a reciprocal arrangement with the other four clubs whereby you were allowed in upon production of the appropriate membership card.

As pleasant as the club was, the major snag was that it had no car park, so you had to park a considerable distance away. I wasn't a sailor, so the Yacht Club, apart from its fairly remote location way down on the east coast of the island, was not really a viable option.

That left the two clubs out at Saar, not too far from the entrance to the Saudi Causeway - The Bahrain Rugby Club and the Dilmun Club. They were both vibrant, well supported clubs with a number of restaurants, bars, swimming pools and in the case of the Dilmun Club, stables. The big plus was that they were both located beyond the urban sprawl of Manama and each had extensive parking. I already knew a few members of the Dilmun Club and I had enjoyed the ambience when I had been there as a visitor, so I opted to join that one and it was to become the focus of much of my social life over the next nine years.

The clubs were far from being the only options available on an island where entertainment and hospitality had become one of the major growth industries and a chief source of national income. A multitude of hotels had been built over the previous twenty years. These included many luxurious five-star establishments as well as three and four star hotels which catered for those on lower budgets.

The venerable Delmon Hotel in the heart of Manama, which I had visited some twenty-five years earlier on my dhow trip, had become a little jaded with the passage of time. The bars at the rear now catered for more downmarket tastes. Belly-dancers performed to Arabic music in one area, while the dubious Diggers Bar hosted Filipino bands playing loud rock music and which was filled each evening with dozens of Chinese prostitutes for whom there were many eager takers.

I had been surprised upon my return to Bahrain to see how a hitherto fairly straight-laced Islamic society had been transformed into a liberal, freewheeling place where prostitution and the conspicuous consumption of alcohol was very visible. Bars such as Diggers were not present in all hotels, most of the upmarket establishments would not countenance such activities, but those hotels with a three-star rating or lower, had a reputation for this kind of thing and it was all done under the knowing and watchful eyes of the authorities.

Bahrain had changed primarily because its income from oil had been in decline for decades and the opening of the causeway in 1986 had led to a surge of visitors from Saudi Arabia - locals and expatriates alike - for whom Bahrain was a place to let off steam and have a good time. It has often been described as Saudi Arabia's very own pressure relief valve. Whatever the reason for this change, the choices of entertainment were now endless. Restaurants serving almost any type of cuisine could be found, from Mexican to Japanese and Indian to Italian. Bars, many of which were themed like Irish, Australian, American or British dotted the island. Discotheques and live music could be found everywhere.

Adding to this demand for entertainment was the fact that Bahrain had, since the First Gulf War some fifteen years earlier, become home to a large naval presence. It now hosted the United States Navy 5th fleet as well as other NATO navies with the Royal Navy also having a sizeable presence. There was therefore, both a permanent and visiting number of military personnel on the island eager for entertainment.

As part of its plan to become the entertainment capital of the Gulf, Bahrain had entered the world of international motor sport with the opening of the Formula One circuit at Sakhir in the southern part of the island. It had been an enormous investment to turn a barren patch of desert sand into the Bahrain International Circuit - a world class race track complete with state of the art grandstands and other facilities. Motor racing was not my first love in sport, but it was undeniably a magnificent circus and once hooked, I attended virtually all of the races from 2006 until 2014.

An additional bonus to living in Bahrain was that my wife and daughter could visit at any time without requiring a visa in advance, a ninety day visa being routinely issued to British passport holders upon arrival at the airport. Many of my friends from the UK were also keen to visit me and see what the place had to offer.

I recall that some friends came to visit not long before the Bahrain grand prix. We had gone out for brunch on a Friday and though I was driving, had probably had enough glasses of sparkling wine to put me over the limit. Nevertheless there was to be a parade of vintage racing cars on the corniche and when we had finished our meal I drove them down to see the spectacle.

On the way there, I made a wrong turn on a traffic island, stopped and reversed. Unfortunately I reversed into the bumper of the car behind me. It was a very low speed collision, but conscious of the fact I was almost certainly over the limit, I sped off with the car following me in hot pursuit and honking his horn. I raced through the backstreets of Manama shouting at my friend's wife sat in the back, to lie down as her blond hair would make my otherwise nondescript car easily identifiable to my pursuer. She claimed later that it was like being in a James Bond movie. Eventually, satisfied that I had shaken him off, I pulled into a car park. As I opened my door, a car screeched to a halt behind me. Damn!

A young Bahraini got out of the car and shouted that I had failed to stop after hitting his vehicle. I claimed that I hadn't realised there had been any contact, but I examined his car and noted that there was a slight dent in the bumper and bodywork below. The last thing I wanted him to do was call the police who would almost certainly breathalyse me. I offered profuse apologies for my mistake and pulled out my wallet. I took out two hundred Bahraini dinars, equivalent to about three hundred pounds. 'Will this be enough to cover it?' I ventured. 'Oh no' he replied, 'That's too much, it will only cost about a hundred dinars to repair'!!! Where else in the world would that happen?

My new employer worked exclusively for Saudi Aramco, performing small packages of detailed design work as a smaller part of bigger projects. The idea of sub-contracting this type of work had been an Aramco initiative to develop an in-Kingdom design capability. This was laudable enough goal and one in keeping with Aramco's business ethos of promoting local business wherever possible. The reality of it however, was that local businessmen, often former Aramco employees, set up these companies and obtained contracts by recruiting foreign engineers and designers.

Very few of the engineers employed by these companies were Saudis. The design contracts were managed by the same organisation within Aramco where I had previously been employed so I had an intimate knowledge of the way they worked. This fact had not been lost upon the owner of the company who had hired me.

Having spent fifteen years at Aramco it seemed odd to be now sitting on the opposite side of the table to what was now the client. Comparisons between elephants and mice spring to mind when comparing the size of Aramco, the largest oil company in the world, with the myriad of smaller service companies which sought to do business with them. Within the contractor community there seemed to be an aura about the large and powerful Aramco which was interesting to witness from 'outside the circle'.

My former employer had continued to evolve during the eleven years I was away. In addition to the executive management, nearly all the senior and middle ranking managerial positions were now occupied by Saudi Arabs. Most of them had been to various universities in the United States, or Europe and were highly motivated and eager to rise up the corporate chain. They all spoke fluent English albeit with an American accent as it was in the United States where it had invariably been learnt.

I had many occasions to meet with our client. Some of their representatives I knew from my time there, others I had not met before though it was always entertaining when I casually mentioned that I had worked for Aramco for fifteen years. Sometimes their reaction appeared to be one of fear, possibly of the fact that I might actually know more than they did, or that I personally knew someone higher up the chain of command.

It was true that many Saudi Arab employees I had known eleven years earlier in low and medium level positions had now been promoted to senior executive positions. I had opportunities to use this to my advantage on a few occasions.

Apart from contracts management I was also responsible for human resources and therefore recruitment. The employment of foreign nationals in Saudi Arabia had always depended upon the obtaining of visas from the Ministry of Labour. It was not possible to obtain single visas, so periodically, companies would apply for a number of visas which were called block visas. Applications for these had to be applied for months in advance of any recruitment activity.

It was quite possible that the number applied for might be

arbitrarily reduced by the Ministry of Labour, part of whose objective was to ensure that Saudi Arabs were given priority for jobs. Although this was a laudable objective, it was a problematic process as the visas which comprised up the block were firstly expensive and secondly, had to specify the nationality and the job title. This was somewhat limiting as it was not always possible to match the job title with the nationality and this led to some unusual situations.

One of our employees was Ashok, an Indian engineer with Canadian citizenship. He was a former Aramco employee and had been for twenty-five years until his retirement from that company. He had been hired by us on an 'in-Kingdom transfer' which avoided having to use one of our precious block visas. It was only upon the completion of this process that we discovered, as did he, that when he'd been hired as an engineer by Aramco some two decades earlier, they had put his job title as 'Food Nutritionist'. They had obviously put him against one of their unused visas. His Aramco job title was Engineer, but as far as the Saudi government was concerned, he would forever be a food nutritionist.

In order to apply for a block visa, the government required information regarding the size of the existing workforce and the ratio of foreign to Saudi staff. The number of visas granted would be based upon this ratio, so the greater the number of Saudis the more likely the visa was to be approved. This led to the widespread employment of locals in what could be termed 'non-jobs'. They weren't really needed and they turned up whenever they felt like it and didn't do an awful lot even when they were there. Nevertheless it bumped up the Saudi numbers and made the approval of a new block visa more likely.

As part of my duties as human resources manager, I was also nominally in charge of government affairs activities. In reality this was a purely Saudi affair and the manager of this small unit, Abdullah was in fact the nephew of one of the Saudi co-owners and pretty much reported directly to him rather than to me. He and his staff of three had to liaise with government departments on all official matters, visas, passports, driving licences etc.

One of Abdullah's three young staff members was Naif, a very personable young man who wore his hair quite long, not something you saw very often in Saudi Arabia other than in the Bedouin. I received a phone call one afternoon from the manager of another company in Al Khobar saying that one of our vehicles with the company logo on the door, had been involved in a serious accident outside his premises and that the driver had been taken to the Al Mana hospital. He gave me the car number and after checking, I found that it was assigned to Naif. The phone call ended with him saying 'it was bad... really bad.'

I summoned Abdullah to tell him and he quickly left for the hospital. It transpired that a vehicle had pulled out in front of Naif with no warning and he had been unable to avoid a collision. He was as usual, exceeding the speed limit and not wearing a seat belt. Abdullah returned to the office a few hours later to tell me that Naif had sustained serious head injuries and was in a coma.

Saudis habitually failed to wear seat belts, perhaps they felt them to be restrictive, but more likely it was due to their fatalistic outlook on life. God would decide if and when it was your time to die and nothing and no-one could prevent that. Naif was now comatose. I went to visit him the following day with Abdullah. He lay on the bed connected to multiple tubes and wires. His apparently lifeless body would twitch every few minutes, but otherwise there were no signs of life.

As Abdullah drove us back to the office in sombre mood, I noted that he was not wearing his belt as usual and idly commented that perhaps if Naif had been wearing one, he might not have been so seriously injured. Abdullah merely shrugged.

The following morning Abdullah came to see me and informed me that Naif had died during the night and that the funeral would be held later that day. 'It was his time' was all he said. At twenty-two, married and with a young child, it seemed to me to be anything other than 'Naif's time'. I didn't go to the funeral in Qatif as it would not have been appropriate for a non-Muslim to attend prayers in the mosque.

Chapter 26

Ladies in the Workforce

By 2006 things were changing in Saudi Arabia. King Abdullah had decreed that women would be allowed to work provided that it was done in accordance with Islamic principles, but quite what these exactly were in the context of twenty first century working practices was anyone's guess. The General Manager at the company was a Muslim Lebanese and a worldly man who felt that the change in the law could be used to our advantage. He also believed that it was about time the country was dragged into the modern age and instructed me to set about hiring ten Saudi females.

Although Aramco had employed females, including Saudi females for many years, they were the sole exception in the business life of the Kingdom. Outside of Aramco, Saudi women were only permitted to work either in girls' schools or in womens' hospitals. It is hard then, to overstate the change in concept for an ordinary Saudi company to begin employing females when it had hitherto been one hundred percent staffed by men. This would be a sea-change of epic proportions.

Having ladies on the payroll would help in securing new block visas as the formula applied by Ministry of Labour took into account the percentage of Saudi employees. Females and disabled employees counted double in this calculation, so the Saudization percentage would be increased by more than the overall number employed.

Employment of Saudi ladies was undoubtedly a progressive move. It was all very well for the management to proceed with this plan, but what about the rest of the workforce? The employees, as in most companies in that part of the world, had only ever worked in a male only environment. We would soon find out.

As head of human resources, I would be the one to put this idea into motion, although in fairness, the general manager said that he would also like to participate in all interviews and in the selection process. We didn't really have any vacancies and weren't entirely sure either what the calibre, or educational attainments of the applicants might be…if indeed we had any. This was unchartered territory and the search for suitable candidates began with the Saudi Ladies Chamber of Commerce who kept a list of all lady graduates who had expressed an interest in finding a job.

They sent us around fifty CVs and out of these we shortlisted a group of candidates. All the applicants were graduates, all were in the age range of twenty-one to thirty and unsurprisingly, none of them had any work experience whatsoever. It was time to see what they were like and accordingly, interviews were arranged. We did not anticipate that any of the young ladies would be attending the interviews alone and so it proved.

The candidates were always accompanied at the interview by a protective father, brother and on one occasion a husband. The girls generally spoke excellent English and were all from good and sometimes prominent families who clearly had a liberal and progressive attitude towards female advancement and within reason, had no objection to their daughters going out to work. It was clear that these intelligent, young women craved an opportunity to leave their gilded cages at home and venture into the wider world. Nearly all had degrees in interior design, one of the few subjects they were able to study at the various female universities in the kingdom.

Quite how we could put interior designers to work in an engineering company remained to be seen, but we pressed on regardless. The interview process was one of the most entertaining and enlightening endeavours I have ever undertaken at work. They were held in the company's main conference room, but it was surprising how many of the staff in the building, happened to be passing along that corridor just as the candidates arrived.

The normal Arabic pleasantries were exchanged as the young lady and her guardian entered. After a few minutes, it became clear that rather than us interviewing the young lady, the general manager and I were actually being interviewed by the girl's father. Their concerns naturally, were that their daughters would be respected and treated well, rather than any questions about what their role was likely to be. When their prospective position in the organisation was explained, they were more relaxed knowing that they would probably be reporting to an expatriate, either myself, or another manager rather than to a Saudi. This perhaps explains much about the local psyche.

I vaguely knew the father of one of the interviewees from my days at Aramco, where he still worked. His relief was palpable when I told him that his daughter would be working for me. 'You are a good man,' he said. 'I know that you will treat my daughter like your own' and of course I assured him that I would.

There was just one young lady who turned up for the interview unescorted. Her name was Maha. For some reason on this occasion, I was conducting the interview alone. She strode confidently into the interview room and closed the door behind her. Clad entirely in black, she proceeded not only to remove her face covering, but also to her headscarf and *habiyah,* revealing long, lustrous locks of dyed fair hair and a heavily made up face. 'I like to get rid of this nonsense whenever I can,' she announced as she sat down.

I swiftly got up and re-opened the door, making the excuse that it was a little stuffy in the room. You could never be too careful. She interviewed well, spoke good English and clearly had bucket loads of personality, but something told me that she might not be an ideal fit. This was after all something of an experiment and we were really looking for girls with perhaps 'less attitude'…… at least initially, until we gauged the reaction of our other employees to this change.

The interview process was completed and eight job offers were made. I would be taking three of the girls into my department, Nadia, Lulu and Fatimah. I made a separate large office available with three desks within the largely open plan floor. The office was fully glazed, but had venetian blinds inside. They were all sweet girls, eager to learn and to make a contribution. Their attitude was a refreshing change from many of their male compatriots whom it must be said, didn't always have the greatest work ethic.

The ladies were of course driven to the office every morning, usually by the family driver. They would come into my office first thing every morning to greet me, often bringing some sweet delicacies from their home, sometimes locally grown dates if they were in season.

Of all the girls we hired, only one proved to be something of a disappointment. She was a slightly older lady in her late thirties who had attended the interview wearing an *habiyah* and just like all the other candidates had left her face uncovered. She would be working on the reception desk in the main entrance area, but within a week of starting, she started to wear a full veil.

This was not exactly the modern, progressive image we were trying to portray to the visitors and guests at a modern go-ahead company. What to do? There was no way that anyone could realistically instruct a Saudi lady to remove her veil and it was certainly not going to be a heathen foreigner like myself.

The general manager and I discussed transferring her to a less prominent job, but when she was approached on the subject, she made it clear that she was only prepared to work on the reception desk. The owner was consulted on the matter, but he said that it was no problem leaving her where she was. She was a lady and despite being veiled, would still demonstrate that the company was moving in the right direction. She therefore stayed where she was and fortunately none of the other girls followed suit, thankfully leaving their faces unveiled when in the office.

The issue of veils was an interesting one. The activities of the *Mutawain*, or religious police had been somewhat reigned in during the past decade and they were less active than they had been years previously. It was increasingly left to the individual, or her husband, or father to determine whether or not they should be fully veiled. Generally the older the lady the more she was likely to wear a full veil and in some cases a leather mask. Younger women and teenage girls often left their faces uncovered.

Restaurants in Saudi Arabia had long been segregated into separate areas, one for families and one for bachelors. These areas were sometimes different rooms, or sections of a larger room separated by curtains. Occasionally when I accompanied my wife to a restaurant in Al Khobar and was seated in the family section, I was always amused at the sight of ladies continually lifting their veils in order to put each spoonful of food into their mouths before dropping the veil once again.

Chapter 27

Getting Restless

I was beginning to find work a little frustrating. Despite the statements of the owner that he wished to expand the company, he seemed unwilling to invest any money in doing so. It really wasn't going anywhere and it seemed to me that he would forever be content to live off the scraps thrown its way by Aramco.

I had been with the company almost eighteen months when I began to look around for a new opportunity. Having already made the move back to the Gulf it was logical to seek a new challenge there and besides, I had plenty of contacts. In fact it was a former colleague at Aramco during a casual conversation at the Dilmun Club one evening who asked me how things were going at work. I replied that things weren't great and that I was looking to make a move.

I had known him for many years and he'd left Aramco some years back to move to one of the largest construction companies in Saudi Arabia where he had risen to the position of Vice-President. He had been having difficulties of his own with the CEO there and wanted to leave, but had agreed to find someone to replace him, or at least assume some of his responsibilities. He wondered if I might be interested in taking on the contract management side of his role. This was certainly my field and I indicated that I would be very interested and he said that he would arrange an interview with the CEO.

The company was one of the venerable Saudi construction companies which had begun life back in the 1950s to support some of Aramco's earliest operations. As the oil industry had expanded, so had this company, evolving over the decades into one of the largest contractors in the kingdom with activities which included steel fabrication factories, heavy lift capability and a fleet of twelve vessels to support offshore construction projects. It had a workforce of around twenty thousand scattered across multiple sites throughout the kingdom.

The company headquarters were located in the city of Dammam and it was there I made my way one sweltering hot day in May of 2007. The CEO was a Christian Lebanese who had been a politician in his home country, at one time holding a ministerial position. He was also something of an old rogue. We met and chatted in his plush and expansive office over Arabic coffee and Lebanese pastries.

As ever, the fact that I had worked for many years in Aramco was considered a huge advantage, particularly as most of their projects were in the oil and gas sector where Aramco was usually the client. The chat, rather than a formal interview was over and we went straight down the hall to the office of the Vice President of human resources whom he instructed to make me a 'good offer'.

We shook hands, he went off and I was made the offer then and there. It was double my existing salary and what's more it promised to be an exciting position, but nevertheless I said I would give it some consideration over the next twenty-four hours. I had learned over many years in Arabia that it doesn't pay to appear too eager. Of course there was no way I was going to turn the offer down, but didn't give him a call until later the following afternoon to say that I would accept.

All that remained now was to hand in my notice. I decided to not to reveal that I had another job and when I spoke to the general manager merely explained the reasons why I hadn't been happy for some time. He understood, but asked that I go and speak to the owner myself since I had been hired by him in the first place. This I did, thanking him for the opportunity that he had given me, but outlining the various reasons why I felt I was wasting my time and wasting his money. I knew that the latter part of this sentiment would lay close to his heart.

He didn't appear surprised, merely shrugged and wished me well. I didn't ask him for a Letter of No Objection which would have allowed me to transfer employment within the kingdom as I did not wish to share this information. I worked my month's notice and got ready to temporarily depart the country to commence a new visa application process in the UK. This would take a couple of weeks and would allow me to spend some time at home.

The three young Saudi ladies who worked for me were quite upset when they heard I was leaving. In the nine months they had been working in my department, they had looked up to me as some kind of re-assuring father figure and they were a little apprehensive about who would be their next boss.

This small matter had still not been decided even upon my last day of work. Nadia in particular seemed the most upset and was in floods of tears as we bade each other farewell later that afternoon. I dearly wanted to give her a hug, but remembered where I was and restrained myself. I found out later that many of the girls we had hired, left the company during the following twelve months.

I had made it clear to my new employer that I would continue to live in Bahrain and commute daily, in fact the CEO lived in Bahrain himself, so there was no problem and no need to terminate my existing apartment rental or make any new domestic arrangements. I flew back to the UK for a few weeks during the pleasant month of June, while my passport was sent to the Royal Saudi Consulate in London for the new visa.

Chapter 28

A New Challenge

Within ten days the visa was granted and it was time to return. I flew to Bahrain and was picked up at my apartment the following morning by one of the company drivers and taken over the causeway to Saudi Arabia and the office in Dammam. My company assigned car and office were waiting for me there. I was introduced to my staff and to the rest of the management team.

It was quite an operation, on a completely different and far grander scale than that of my last employer. About 300 people worked in the headquarters, a four-storey concrete and glass building in the heart of the city. It was just around the corner from 'Chop Chop Square' where the public executions took place.

The company, like the rest of the country, was involved in another era of great expansion. When I had first arrived in Saudi Arabia almost thirty years earlier, it had been on the wave of unprecedented high oil prices and the desire to capture and utilise the previously wasted resource of natural gas. This time, the focus was on the development of further downstream operations involving the conversion of gas and oil into a variety of products - polypropylene, polyethylene, ammonia fertilisers, sulphur, high density polyethylene piping and so forth.

They were perfectly poised to take advantage of this expansion program having all the infrastructure in place; accommodation camps, vehicles, cranes, heavy equipment, a fleet of offshore supply and support vessels as well as steel fabrication factories. The wave of expansive optimism in the 2005 - 2007 period, shortly before the global financial crisis had also created the perfect environment in which the owners decided to embark on a stock market flotation.

It would be the first construction company in Saudi Arabia to do so and, apart from potentially producing a huge windfall profit for the owners, would make a powerful statement that this was no longer an old-fashioned company. It would henceforth be a public limited company with shares traded on the nascent Saudi Stock Exchange, the *Tadawul.*

In order for a successful Initial Public Offering (IPO) to take place, there needed to be a full order book and obtaining new contracts at this time was the order of the day. Aramco was still the big beast in the country and contracts directly with them were highly sought after. Aramco however was entering into joint ventures with other global players in the oil and gas sector, not just the traditional European and American companies, but increasingly with newer players in the field from Asia; Japan, South Korea and particularly China.

Many of the larger joint venture projects would be sub-divided into separate components, the detailed design and construction of each part would then be awarded on a competitive basis. Gone were the days when this would be heavily dominated by American giants such as Fluor, Parsons and Bechtel. The market was now dominated by companies such as Mitsui, Samsung, Hyundai and Sinopec.

The same was true of projects under the auspices of the Saudi Arabian Basic Industries Corporation (SABIC) which oversaw downstream activities. Once again the design and construction packages of these proposed facilities were awarded in the keen competition of the international market and increasingly, these projects were awarded to Asian companies. Some American and European companies managed to retain a competitive edge, particularly in areas of technology where they possessed a particular know-how, for example aluminium production, or seamless pipe making technology.

The industrial base of Saudi Arabia had evolved remarkably over the past thirty years and a wide variety of manufacturing companies had grown up, taking advantage of free land, cheap imported labour, cheap energy and of course an almost free and never-ending source of natural gas, called feedstock.

It was boom time once again and as one of the major players in the Saudi construction market, my new employer was perfectly poised not only to secure its long term future, but to make a killing for the owners in the forthcoming flotation.

In addition to securing new prime contracts, the company had a large number of existing projects spread across the kingdom from east to west all of which, due to their complexity and typical lifespan of two years, required numerous and ongoing contractual discussions. These usually revolved around progress payments, delays and design changes. A signed contract at the start of such a project was merely a map and not the definitive final journey.

As well as the prime contracts, my responsibilities involved the award of multiple sub-contracts to a variety of companies who possessed a particular skill set, or type of equipment which we did not possess, or indeed to fill a gap in capacity when we were overstretched. The number of these contracts were set to increase dramatically. It looked like I was going to be busy.

Apart from the demands of my new job, daily life continued much as before. I lived in the same apartment in Bahrain, commuted daily over the causeway, though in a slightly more up-market company car. The daily commute was a little longer and this was made more arduous because my new company, in line with most contractor companies in Saudi Arabia, worked a six-day week. In reality this was a five and half day week as we usually left the office in the early afternoon. For me this was a particular chore as, in addition to wrestling with long queues every Wednesday evening, I would also have to endure them on Thursday afternoons.

It was around this time that Bahrain and most of the other Gulf states changed their weekends from Thursday and Friday to Friday and Saturday. The rationale was that in commercial dealings with the rest of the world they would only lose two working days per week rather than the three working days lost hitherto. The ever-conservative government of Saudi Arabia did not immediately follow suit and retained the traditional weekend of Thursday and Friday for some time to come. It was a little odd residing in a country with a different weekend to the one I was working in, but in reality it didn't make an awful lot of difference.

My new job was full on from day one and I quickly discovered that in addition to long days in the headquarters office, I would frequently have to travel the length and breadth of Saudi Arabia and beyond. As with all personnel needing access to various Aramco sites, an Aramco Contractor ID was required. There were many levels of security clearance encoded into these cards, specific both to individual facilities and even to certain areas within them. Due to the nature of my job, I had far greater levels of security clearance than I had ever had when I had been an employee of Saudi Aramco.

I got on very well with the CEO, but as I mentioned before, he was something of a rogue, but nevertheless we developed a good working relationship. He had been in charge of the company for two spells, once back in the late seventies and early eighties and then again from 2000 onwards. He was well past the normal retirement age and being in charge of the company leading up to a successful flotation, would be a fitting finale to his career.

He lived in a large villa in Bahrain, right on the edge of Tubli Bay. It was a house built for entertaining and he certainly used it for that purpose. My first visit to the villa after joining the company, was to attend a party being held in honour of the Chief Executive of Samsung - Middle East. It was a lavish affair with tables on the terrace overlooking the water. The Samsung chief executive arrived with four colleagues and was treated to an extravagant meal featuring the most amazing Lebanese cuisine.

I was seated next to the CEO at the head of the table with the Korean on the other side. The object of the exercise was to cement the existing relationship between the two companies as we were already engaged in two ongoing projects which were going well. With the forthcoming flotation we were eager to secure additional projects to augment our project list and achieve as high a share price as possible.

After the meal and fine wine, it was time for Arabic coffee and tea. The CEO summoned over his aide and whispered something in his ear. He scurried away. He returned a few minutes later with two cut glass tumblers each one third full of golden liquid. One was handed to the Samsung executive while my boss was handed the other one. He then stood up and proposed a toast to our distinguished Korean guest and the liquid was downed in one by both men.

Further glasses were brought and another toast was made to the continued alliance of the two companies, again followed by the downing of the contents in a single gulp. While the next tumblers were being brought, he leaned over to me and said, 'the Korean's glass is filled with Scotch, mine is filled with cold tea' and winked.

Sure enough new glasses were brought and the Korean was invited to propose a toast of his own which courtesy demanded. By the conclusion of the fifth toast, the Korean was having difficulty standing and shortly thereafter slumped forward with his head on the table - Asians I had observed before, generally do not take their liquor well.

It was clearly time to bring the festivities to an end and the four Samsung executives had to take their CEO, one on each limb and carry him out to his waiting car. My boss had arranged for all this to be secretly filmed in case 'it might come in handy' at some point in the future.

Unethical though he was I had a sneaking admiration for him. He sailed close to the wind on many occasions, but he certainly knew how to strike a deal and had a presence in any room.

Chapter 29

The CEO Departs

The CEO's days were coming to a close. The newly floated company would henceforward have a new Saudi CEO and he took over at the end of 2007. It would mark the beginning of a Saudization process which would continue over the next couple of years to a point where all the senior positions in the company apart from my own, would be occupied by Saudi nationals.

I managed to get on fairly well with all the new Saudis who joined the company at that time, but nevertheless felt myself gradually excluded from many management meetings. I had been around long enough not to take this personally and just got on with my job which presumably I was considered to be doing well enough, otherwise I would have undoubtedly been replaced. Apart from that, things seemed to be going well, on the surface at least. Additional contracts were being awarded and in the days before the global financial crisis of 2008, the share price was buoyant.

Virtually all contracts were awarded on a competitive tender basis and naturally, our pricing had to be on the mark. Estimation and tendering were not part of my remit and I would review only the contractual terms and conditions. It would only later become apparent that we had been a little too aggressive in the pricing on some of these projects and would struggle to make a profit. I recall that early in 2009, I went on a business trip with the new CEO.

We had been shortlisted by a potential client, an international steel company based in Luxembourg and travelled there hoping to finalise the deal to build a new steel factory in Jubail. I didn't really have a huge role to play in the proceedings as I had already reviewed the contract and reached a preliminary agreement on the text. The only thing that remained to be agreed was the price.

The Saudis often liked to take a westerner along because they felt, as one once told me, 'that we need to show the client that we are not just a bunch of camel jockeys.'

We went out for dinner in the old part of the city the night before the meeting. The CEO said that we should order some champagne before the meal to celebrate what would surely be another contract award the following day. He nodded at me and said that he didn't know too much about champagne, but that we should order a good one. I looked at the wine list and plumped for the most expensive bottle of Krug on the list. It was three hundred and fifty Euros and he never batted an eyelid. It would be put on expenses after all.

After the champagne and a few bottles of fine wine, tongues became a little looser and discussion of the contract price took place. Pricing was always carried out under a typically Arabian shroud of secrecy, so I only had a rough idea of what the lump sum price offer was likely to be.

I guessed from the work scope of the project that our bid price would be in the region of two hundred and fifty million

Saudi riyals, the equivalent of seventy five million dollars and assumed that our contingencies, for there were always contingencies, together with our mark-up would mean that our costs to complete would be in the region of two hundred million Saudi riyals, the equivalent of sixty million dollars. The CEO turned to me and said that it was important that we were awarded this particular contract and that he was prepared to reduce the price in order to get it. He then wrote a figure on a napkin, turned it over and asked me how low I thought our minimum price could go.

I guessed at two hundred million riyals which in my opinion would allow us to breakeven with the possibility of a small profit should things go well. He then turned over the napkin to reveal a figure of one hundred and twenty million riyals, the equivalent of thirty five million dollars. Unbelievable! Our direct costs alone, in my opinion, would easily exceed that figure. I must have looked surprised, but he said that they had taken account of all contingencies, delays etc. I hoped he was right, but I suspected that he was not. There was no way we could build the planned facility for anything close to that sum.

Sadly, the seeds of such cavalier disregard for the normal rules of economics would slowly and inevitably produce a bitter harvest. The company had not always made a profit on its various projects, but had largely done so and had therefore been able to subsidise one or two loss making ventures with its more profitable ones. Crucially it had been able to keep sensitive pricing information in house when it had traded as a solely owned private company. It was now publicly limited and the annual financial results would be available to investors as well as to the wider public.

Ras Tanura is Saudi Arabia's main crude oil export terminal, located on the Gulf coast some sixty miles north of Dhahran. In former times piers had been built to accommodate the relatively small tankers which used to load up and transport the oil to customers all over the world. As time went by and export volumes increased, so did the size of oil tankers. It became necessary therefore to build new terminal facilities which stretched out further into deeper water to accommodate the draught of the Very Large Crude Carriers (VLCCs) and the subsequent and even more gargantuan, Ultra Large Crude Carriers (ULCCs) some of which weighed in at a colossal 500,000 tonnes.

A line of man-made structures called Sea Islands, connected by a trestle was constructed about a mile offshore where the sandy bottom shelved away to deeper water. The larger tankers would berth alongside these and underwater pipelines would bring the oil from storage tanks ashore to be pumped aboard.

Due to its vital nature both for the economy of Saudi Arabia and for the stability of global oil prices in general, this was probably the most heavily guarded and protected industrial location in the entire country. Miles of razor wire, hundreds of security cameras and security lighting surrounded the export refinery, storage tanks and any access to the piers or Sea Islands. Not only was the complex guarded by Aramco's own security personnel, but also by the Saudi Coastguard who had fast patrol boats and armoured vehicles at all access points.

The company had secured a project to upgrade and renovate the Sea Islands and on many occasions I had to go and visit the client, occasionally going out by boat to inspect the ongoing works. One sultry August afternoon I drove up to Ras Tanura for a site meeting and started the convoluted process of entering the facility through the three separate security cordons. Producing my ID and signing a visitor register had to be completed at each one and then at the third and final entrance gate, I found the barrier already raised and, thinking that I had been casually waved through by the coastguard, continued driving.

I had only driven a few yards down the road, when I heard shouts and saw in my rear-view mirror a camouflaged soldier waving his arms. More worryingly, I heard the heavy machine gun on the armoured vehicle which was parked adjacent to the entrance gate being cranked around to point in my direction. I hit the brakes fearing that my car and me, might shortly be given a new air-conditioning system!

Slowly getting out of the car with hands raised, I walked back to the checkpoint. What I had mistaken for a lazy wave through in the stultifying heat of an August afternoon, had in fact been an instruction to halt. I produced my ID once again and apologised profusely for my mistake before I was eventually allowed to continue on my way. I was thankful that the coastguard had not opted for the shoot first and ask questions later approach although this would not be the last time that I found myself in the gunsights of a heavy armoured vehicle.

It was a few months later that I had to fly to the west coast. It was Ramadan and as my Muslim boss was fasting, he asked me at very short notice if I would mind going in his place to meet with one of our clients. I wasn't particularly keen to travel during Ramadan either as I knew there would be precious little open during the hours of daylight, but nevertheless agreed to go. It was more convenient to fly from Bahrain to Jeddah, so my secretary booked the flights. I would only be there a couple of days, how bad could it be?

In addition to the great *haj* pilgrimage to Mecca, Muslims from around the world make the *umra* or lesser pilgrimage at different times of the year. One of the most popular of these times is during the month of Ramadan, though the principle remains basically the same regarding prayers and visiting the various holy places.

The principal port of entry for those arriving by air is the King Abdulaziz International Airport in Jeddah. Pilgrims are processed in the *Haj Terminal,* a vast complex at the farthest extremity of the airport. This was well away from the regular arrival and departure terminals which would otherwise have been overloaded with these mass arrivals.

I had been unable to get a business class seat on Gulf Air, due to the lateness of the booking. As the rest of the passengers boarded I immediately noticed two things; one, that the flight was full and two, that without exception, the other passengers all appeared to be from the Indian sub-continent and were all wearing the two garment pilgrim *ihram* robes which look much the same as large white fluffy towels. Two hours was going to be an awfully long time.

After ten minutes it became clear that none of them had ever flown before, apart from the flight they must have taken to reach Bahrain and that they could neither read nor write English. It was also becoming increasingly apparent that they hadn't had a shower for a number of days.

They had no clue how to find their allocated seats and still less of an idea how to stow their baggage in the overhead lockers. Time was running on and the cabin staff were at their wits' end, eventually resorted to shouting and pushing some of the men down into the nearest seat. We were already thirty minutes late taking off and in danger of losing our slot.

Eventually, we were ready for take-off. I buried my nose in a book and pretended that the pandemonium around me wasn't really happening. About thirty minutes after take-off, the pilgrim sitting next to me started fidgeting in his small hand bag. He eventually fished out his Saudi landing card, but seemed perplexed as what to do with it. Seemingly he also had no pen. After a few minutes he nudged me and indicated that perhaps I might be able to lend him a hand in filling it out.

I sighed, put down my book and taking his passport, began to fill in the various boxes of the card. My act of kindness was witnessed by all those seated around and when his was complete, I had a steady line of passengers requiring the same service. When I had filled in thirty or forty of these I had to call a halt and resumed reading my book.

We would be commencing our descent in about half an hour and I could at last disembark. Sure enough the captain throttled back the engines and we began to lose altitude. The rocky western escarpment of the Hejaz mountains was directly below us and the sapphire blue, Red Sea stretched away in the distance.

We made a smooth landing and, despite the admonishments of the cabin crew, many of the pilgrims immediately stood up while the aircraft was still in motion and began emptying their belongings from the overhead lockers. It was a wonder some of them weren't injured, but I suppose Allah would have been protecting them.

The plane continued to taxi, but not to the international terminal, we were headed slowly, but surely towards the *Haj Terminal*. This I knew, would be filled chaotically with thousands more identically clad pilgrims, just like the ones on board. The engines were cut as the plane stopped alongside the cavernous terminal, more of an open-air affair covered by vast canvas canopy, the size of ten football fields to protect the occupants from the sun. My misery was complete.

Fortunately, a member of the cabin crew, aware of my plight, informed me that I would be taken by car to the regular international terminal.

If the scenes were chaotic upon arrival, they were no better when I departed a couple of days later. Although I was thankfully in the international terminal, a number of pilgrims were also catching planes from here. The check-in area was a sea of white as men jockeyed for position at each check-in counter. Their luggage on the outbound journey now augmented by numerous, large plastic jerry-cans. These were filled with holy *Zamzam* water taken from the spring in Mecca, supposedly containing all kinds of beneficial properties, both spiritual and physical. These heavy containers were lugged onto the check-in scales and tagged by the airline staff as if this were quite normal... which of course it was. I made a mental note never again to fly to Jeddah during Ramadan.

If further evidence were needed of the disastrous way the company was now being directed, we were gradually turning away from our proven capability in the oil and gas sector. We had bid and been awarded a civil contract with Binladen

Corporation for a portion of the construction of the King Abdullah University of Science & Technology (KAUST) being constructed on a coastal site near the small town of Thuwal, fifty miles north of Jeddah. The fact that we had neither the type of manpower to perform this work, or that we had no labour camp anywhere in the area, was deemed by the executive management at that time not to be a problem.

Hiring manpower, or transferring five-hundred workers from other projects wouldn't be too difficult, but accommodating them in just a couple of months might be a little trickier. Naturally, a company the size of ours had a department which operated the running of all our labour camps throughout the kingdom and had done so for decades. So who did the company put in charge of finding this accommodation on the west coast? Yours truly.

Although I had visited Jeddah a few times, I didn't know the city very well, much less the location and availability of any accommodation suitable for five-hundred workers. The reason I had been given this task was purely because the Saudi executives believed that I would do the job honestly and wouldn't cut any side-deals with potential suppliers. I was provided with a Saudi assistant with some local knowledge as it was clear that my limited Arabic wouldn't allow me to complete the task alone.

So off we went to Jeddah for a week. I checked into the fabulous Park Hyatt Hotel located right on the waterfront, fabulous in every respect except that it didn't have a bar. We had some maps of the city and environs and began to look at logistics. The most obvious option was to find somewhere in Thuwal, but failing that, it would have to be somewhere closer in to the city. Anything further away would be a logistical nightmare with the appalling traffic congestion throughout the city.

The next day we took a drive up to Thuwal to find that it was literally a one horse town - a one camel town at any rate. Although the new university complex would be on the doorstep, Thuwal itself comprised only a gas station with a small convenience store, a few desultory mosques, a ramshackle collection of huts and a scattering of incomplete concrete houses. Those contractors who had been involved in the KAUST project from the start would have had the luxury to mobilise and build their own camps from scratch. We asked the obvious questions and checked to see whether any of them might have spare capacity for the odd five-hundred souls, but we were repeatedly given the message that there was no room at the inn... not the first time that phrase had been uttered in the Middle East!

It would therefore have to be Jeddah and so the following day we began the rounds of agents and companies who might be able to help. There were plenty of apartment blocks available, but none could take more than a hundred and fifty men which would mean scattering the workforce across multiple sites with all the logistical problems this would entail for transport, food and laundry etc.

The search went on for another two days without yielding any positive results. Ahmad my assistant, was however a resourceful individual and although from the Eastern Province himself, knew something of the Jeddah locale and had heard of a camp located on the northern side of the city out beyond the airport on the Medina road. We drove out there the following day. The location was promising as it was outside the northern suburbs of the city and crucially, transport time to Thuwal would be less than an hour each way.

The camp was in two parts, a very pleasant family camp with single storey villas set in landscaped grounds around a large swimming pool and a not so pleasant, but perfectly adequate, bachelor camp next door. All had reasonable accommodation and adequate communal washing facilities as well as laundry and kitchens. The camp was owned by a couple of brothers who were originally from Bahrain. It was clear that neither camp was fully occupied, in fact they both seemed largely empty.

Despite all the construction activity around the kingdom at that time, the property market in Jeddah had been in the doldrums for a couple of years. Larger companies tended to build their own camps close to a project and it was only ourselves who had got involved at the tail end of a project who required an already existing facility. It was not the way the company normally operated, but beggars couldn't be choosers. Accommodation charges for regular labour was usually priced on a man per day basis and I had a fair idea of what the rate should be.

The two brothers were charming and insisted that Ahmed and I stay for lunch. The last thing I expected was for one of them to ask whether we would like red or white wine with our meal. I thought he was joking, but he grinned and said that we would not have to drink water as they had been making their own wine on the compound for years as it was highly appreciated by the European and American residents in the Family camp.

Before I could graciously decline their offer, not wishing

to offend Ahmad's sensibilities, he chirped up like the good Muslim he was and said that a bottle of white wine with lunch would be splendid. We negotiated the daily rate over the very pleasant, if somewhat unexpected meal and shook hands on the deal. I returned to Dammam the following day, notified the CEO that we had a deal and that mobilisation could commence.

Chapter 30

Causeway Blues

When I first joined the construction company in Dammam, I was already a veteran of eighteen months causeway commuting. That was a total of six hundred causeway crossings in each direction and to say that it was sometimes tedious, was to put it mildly. In the mornings I would sail through and drive across the sapphire blue sea on the ribbon of grey tarmac and think quite rightly, that this must be one of the finest and most exotic commutes anywhere in the world, but equally in the evenings it would be a mind-numbing chore.

Fellow commuters would exchange horror stories of just how far back from the border controls the queues would begin, or stories of how they had queued for an hour or so in a particular line only for the booth to close while the duty officer either went to pray, was at the end of his shift, or just got fed up and took an unauthorised break. No-one was ever going to let you into another line. There were also tales of how the computer system had suddenly gone down and of people being stranded in the no man's land between the two borders, sometimes for many hours.

There was however, a way around this problem. There existed a VIP pass which could be obtained for an annual fee, the equivalent of five hundred pounds. This pass entitled the driver plus his passengers, to go in a separate and much quieter channel, thus avoiding the melee of the regular lanes. On a busy evening this could cut the journey time by over an hour. I knew a few people who had one of these cards and I thought that this might be a wise investment.

As I was formally a resident of Saudi Arabia, the application had to be made to the Saudi authorities so a little artistic licence was required. I obtained a letter in Arabic from my employer stating that I was required to visit Bahrain on an almost daily basis in furtherance of my duties and the application, together with the fee was dispatched.

Rumours were the usual source of news in Arabia and annoyingly, just at the time I submitted my application, there had been some noises about the fees for VIP passes being increased. More worryingly, a story was circulating, that so many passes had been issued during the past few years, that no more would be approved. I would obviously have to wait and see, wait being the operative word.

Months went by and the rumour mill went into overdrive with talk that the fee would now be increased to the equivalent of five thousand pounds. I could see that my recently submitted application was doomed to failure. In typical Saudi style, nothing was ever officially announced, but as sure as night follows day, no further VIP passes were forthcoming. It seemed that my days of queuing on the causeway were destined to continue.

At that point and quite out of the blue, a former colleague Graham, contacted me. He was now working for a Spanish engineering company in Saudi Arabia, but was also living in Bahrain. He was looking to make a change due to a personality conflict with his boss, I also knew that he had a VIP causeway pass.

I had a word with my CEO and explained that my former colleague was available and might be an asset to the company and he expressed an interest in speaking to him. He was in due course made a job offer which he accepted. It looked like my VIP pass situation would be resolved.

My new travel routine was to pick Graham up from his villa, conveniently located a short drive from the causeway and then, upon arriving in the middle of the causeway, rather than heading for the usual lanes, we would take a right turn and enter the VIP lane. This procedure was repeated every morning and evening and I was able to save at least half an hour on normal days and over an hour on busier ones, which was fantastic. Unfortunately, my colleague for various reasons had a relatively short tenure with the company and before the year was out, I was back to travelling economy class once again.

Some months later, I went on vacation for two weeks, meeting my wife and daughter in Tanzania for a safari holiday. Upon my return I discovered, much to my surprise, that my apartment block had been adorned with an enormous banner draped down one side which proclaimed that it was now an office complex. I entered the building and spoke to Mohammed the concierge, who sadly acknowledged that this was the case and that all the tenants had been given two months' notice to quit. I was most disappointed and though it wasn't the most prestigious apartment block on the island in terms of general facilities, it was spacious and more importantly it was very convenient.

After three years living in Bahrain, I now had to begin apartment hunting once again. By now, I knew the island intimately and knew exactly where I wanted to live and where I didn't. The overriding concern as before, was the location in terms of my daily commute. Fortunately there were numerous options available which would fit the bill, so I moved out of the Seef district and across to the other side of the main Sheikh Khalifa bin Salman Highway to an area called Sanabis.

The old village of Sanabis was a Shia enclave, but this block was some distance from the centre, located alongside the main highway. It was a very well appointed three bed apartment on the tenth floor of *Al Jazeera Tower* with extensive views looking south over the island. I wasn't to know that this panoramic view would come in handy in years to come, but more of that later.

By early 2010 things were not going so well the company and they decided to dispense with the services of their first Saudi CEO and appointed an American of Iranian origin. He would enter the building and conduct individual meetings with all the vice-presidents and senior managers - all of whom were Saudis at that time except myself, yet he never once invited me to meet him. After two weeks of this and more intrigued than annoyed, I went up to his office, knocked on the door and introduced myself.

He was shocked that none of my Saudi colleagues had mentioned me, or indeed offered him the opportunity to meet me. I smiled and said, 'All the executives and senior managers in this building were hired by the recently departed CEO… all except me. Perhaps there are things they don't want you to know.'

'And what exactly is there to know?' he replied.

Two hours later I was still laying out my observations of exactly how, why and where the company had gone wrong.

His mission was to change the course of a ship rapidly heading towards the rocks and bring it onto a more stable financial footing. There would be no more low bidding to obtain contracts, costs would be cut and existing projects would be completed, but at minimal cost. He would be the new broom that would sweep everything clean. That started with the removal of most of the existing management and the exodus of the Saudi executives, who had no doubt painted a glowing picture of their own and the company's performance, was swift.

It appeared that I was safe for the time being and he seemed to appreciate the way I worked. He brought in a couple of Americans to oversee and bring some discipline to the on-going projects where many had seen costs spiralling out of control. All seemed to be heading in the right direction, but the company's Achilles heel was about to be inadvertently and horribly exposed.

Like many others, the company had a huge line of credit available from a consortium of seven banks upon which it could call. It had only ever used about a third of the sums nominally available to it, but in an effort to show transparency, the new CEO's laying out of the current financial position, had the effect of making the bankers more nervous than they already were.

The banks, as banks do, applied the brakes. At that point we could quite easily have traded our way back into financial health. The order book was full and with some disciplined project management, many of the projects could at least have been completed at break-even.

The banks however, would have none of it. Concerned that they might never see a penny of the millions they were owed, they turned off the taps…completely. Access to our current accounts was frozen and no monies could be withdrawn unless the banks collectively and specifically authorised a payment. It was turning into a slow-motion train crash.

This was the last thing a company in trouble needed, access to cash based on the significant revenues which were still pouring into the company's coffers, was its life-blood. Huge payments made to suppliers and sub-contractors along with regular salary payments to our own workforce, were the key to survival.

As the months went by, it would get worse… much worse.

Chapter 31

Going 'Too Fast'

For the entire time I worked in Saudi Arabia and lived in Bahrain, I drove a company car which was registered in Saudi Arabia and had Saudi licence plates. I have already mentioned the poor quality of driving in the region, but in more recent times various sanctions had been introduced to try and curb this behaviour. Police patrol cars with speed cameras as well as some fixed cameras were routinely deployed in an attempt to control the generally reckless driving pattern. I must at this point hold my hand up and confess that I was not always a paragon of virtue when it came to my driving habits.

My excuse is that years of driving in that environment undeniably caused a change in my driving behaviour. In the macho world of Arabian driving, you could never for example, wait for anyone to give way at a traffic intersection. In addition to this being interpreted as a sign of weakness, it also indicated that you had all the time in the world, for no-one would ever give way. You had to force your way out, hoping that the other drivers had seen you and would take avoiding action.

Another example was the routine non-observance of speed limits. Most Arabs drive very large, fast cars and they certainly have the roads on which to enjoy them. From simple two lane strips of tarmac running through the desert thirty years ago, there had been a major road building programme and the sands were now criss-crossed by huge three, four and even five lane highways. Once away from the larger cities, it was very easy to press the accelerator down and 'go for it', which I routinely did.

From the offender's point of view, unless there had been some kind of accident, it merely involved the payment of a fine which rarely exceeded the equivalent of one hundred and fifty dollars. There was no system of points on driving licences, or any issues with insurance cover, merely a cash payment either levied on the spot if caught by a patrol officer, or within thirty days if caught on a fixed camera. It was in short, a speeders paradise and most people took full and flagrant advantage and over the years, I gradually adopted the principle of 'when in Rome'.

I had committed a number of speeding offences which were resolved in Saudi Arabia by making an online payment to the police, a fairly painless and relatively inexpensive process. Bahrain was a slightly different matter, the penalty system was broadly the same, but as my car had foreign plates, the only time you could be apprehended for a speeding offence in Bahrain was at the border on the causeway. As you stopped to pick up your customs declaration form, you would be notified that you had a traffic violation and would need to pay the fine at the police station, conveniently located only fifty yards away.

The policeman would show you a dated photograph of your vehicle with registered speed and then request payment of the fine. It was all done very pleasantly, a receipt was issued indicating that the fine had been paid and you were free to proceed and exit the country.

I had gone through this process more times than I can remember, so one morning when my colleague Chris and I were driving to work, I was again informed at the Bahrain customs booth that there was a fine to pay. I turned the car around and drove to the small police station and asked the desk sergeant how much it was. He looked for the file and then uttered the immortal words; 'Oh no! You were going too fast'.

He then informed me that my speed, when photographed by the fixed camera had been 150 kph in a 100 kph zone. Oh dear! 'So what happens now,' I said, putting my wallet away.

'You will have to take a breathalyser test' he replied. I looked again at the photograph and noted that it had been taken three weeks earlier. 'But that was ages ago.' I protested.

'You still have to take the test,' he replied and grabbed a kit from one of the cabinets behind his desk. It was six thirty in the morning and I was driving into work. I was hardly likely to be over the limit at that time, so I blew heartily into the tube.

Unsurprisingly, it proved negative, but with procedures completed for now, he informed me that I would have to go to the main traffic police headquarters. I responded that I wasn't exactly sure where this was, at which point he smiled sweetly and said, 'Don't worry, we'll be taking you.'

'But I have a colleague in my car.'

'OK,' he said. 'You can follow us there.'

They took my passport which I always carried on my international daily commute and followed the police car with blue lights flashing, all the way back from the middle of the causeway to the Bahrain traffic police headquarters at Riffa in the centre of the island. I parked up and, leaving my colleague in the car, followed one of the policemen into the main building where I was asked to take a seat. It was busy even at this hour, but eventually a policeman who had already been given my passport, wrote down some more information.

I wondered when he was going to ask me to pay the fine, but instead he put my passport in his desk drawer and said, 'Please follow the police officer.'

I followed the policeman out of the building and back into the large car park. The only other building I could see lay on the other side of the car park, a two-storey concrete block with barred windows. My heart sank as the policeman led me in that direction. Passing my colleague who was doing the newspaper crossword in the my car, I tapped on the bonnet and indicated that I thought that I was going to be locked up. He looked up, nodded and then resumed the crossword as if this was somehow quite normal.

Sure enough we walked towards the jail block. The policeman took out a large bunch of keys from his pocket and began to unlock the large metal exterior door. He pushed it open and ushered me inside. A corridor, lit only by a few fluorescent lights stretched away into the interior of the building. On either side of the corridor were barred cells which were largely full of young men, most of whom I assumed were Saudis. They shouted loudly and banged on the bars as the policeman and I walked past. My heart sank, I didn't know how long I was going to be here and I didn't particularly wish to share a fetid and overcrowded cell with the a dozen or so inmates.

The policeman must have seen the look of concern on my face as we walked to the end of the corridor and into a small administrative office. He beckoned me in and once I was inside, he locked the door from the outside. Well, I was certainly in jail, but at least I wasn't in a cell.

In addition to holding my passport, they had also taken my mobile phone, so I couldn't make contact with anyone. I sat down in the only chair in the small room and waited. I could still hear shouts from the occupants of the cells outside as I checked my watch every five minutes. Goodness knows how long the men in the cells had been there. After what seemed an eternity, but was in truth was perhaps only forty-five minutes, I heard footsteps approaching. The same policeman unlocked the door and indicated that I was to follow him.

We went outside once again and walked back across the car park to the main administrative building. The desk sergeant handed back my passport together with my mobile phone and said that I would have to appear in court the following Thursday. In the meantime they were going to impound my vehicle.

My protestations that the car was not my own, but a company car, cut no ice and I had to hand over the keys. My colleague had anticipated this event and had made contact with a mutual friend who was able to provide a car and driver to take us over the causeway and into work. We finally arrived in the office around midday. It's amazing what you can cram into a morning when you get up early!

My forthcoming court appearance in a few days' time was occupying my mind. I was fairly sure that the punishment for my crime would only be a fine, but I was equally sure that it was going to be a large one. There was no way I was going to turn up at the court without a wallet full of cash, calculating that either an inability, or unwillingness to pay might result in another visit to that appalling jail.

If the fines were the equivalent of a hundred and fifty dollars for a normal speeding offence, I guessed that it might be double, or even triple this time. I decided that I wouldn't take any chances and turned up at the court with the equivalent of over a thousand dollars in my pocket.

Thursday was the Saudi weekend, so my court appearance would not necessitate taking a day off work. I caught a taxi to the Riffa traffic police headquarters and waited in the same building where I had been taken a few days before. This time however I was shown into a different section where doors into the various courts led off a wide corridor.

I waited on the bench seat outside the door for more than half an hour before a young Bahraini wearing national dress appeared together with a uniformed policeman. They went in through the door and motioned me to follow. I entered the room to discover that rather than a formal courtroom, it was merely a very large carpeted office. A desk occupied one corner and a huge framed photograph of King Hamad hung on one wall.

On the carpet some twenty feet away from the desk a white circle, about a meter in diameter, had been painted on the carpet. I was invited to stand in this circle while the young Bahraini who looked no more than thirty, idly leafed through some papers. I felt like an errant schoolboy who'd been called into the headmaster's study. Eventually he looked up at me and said, 'Why were you driving so fast that day?' I made up some nonsensical story about being late to meet an important client at the airport.

He leaned back in his chair and said, 'We Bahrainis look up to you Europeans to set a good example in matters of driving.

This is not a good example.' I must have looked suitably contrite and merely nodded in agreement. He pulled his chair up to the desk and wrote something on one of the papers in front of him. 'The fine will be a hundred dinars.' he announced. 'Please don't let me see you in court again.' I assured him that he certainly would not and was escorted out of the room by the uniformed policeman. Through the building once again and back to the desk sergeant, I proffered the money - the equivalent of three hundred dollars which he counted carefully and then handed me back the keys to my car which, he said, could be found around the back in the car pound.

I eventually found my white Nissan company saloon car which must have been the least expensive car in the pound, crammed as it was with high-end exotic motors, many of which appeared to have been left untouched for some considerable time. There were Rolls-Royces, Maseratis, Lamborghinis as well as a plethora of Mercedes, Jaguars and BMW, nearly all of them had Saudi plates. The owners had clearly thought that losing their expensive cars was a better alternative than bothering to return and face the music. Anywhere else in the world, the police would have auctioned off these valuable cars, but in Bahrain, they were just left to rot.

As I drove off, I made a mental note; Continue to speed where appropriate, but don't go 'too fast'.

Chapter 32

The Arab Spring

In late 2010, an unusual phenomenon began sweeping across the Arab world. Starting in Tunisia, it began as a protest against human rights abuses, but gradually gained traction in many other countries across north Africa, turning into an attempt to overturn traditional politics across the Arab world.

It was a fairly well-worn joke that the only Arabs who enjoyed democracy and a life free from political oppression, were those Arabs who lived in Israel. From Morocco in the west, to the Arabian peninsula in the east, there was barely a single Arab country that possessed a glimmer of democracy. They were, almost without exception, either absolute monarchies, or military dictatorships.

The rest of the world was intrigued that at last, the Arabs seemed to be wakening from their eternal political slumber and so it was christened 'The Arab Spring'. In Tunisia it had begun over a dispute about police harassment, but it soon spread eastwards, firstly to Libya, then Egypt, on to Syria and finally to Bahrain.

Some of the young Saudis in my department - Shias all, knowing that I lived in Bahrain, would drop hints that there might soon be protests over there. It would be no great surprise, for although the population of Bahrain was predominantly Shia, it was ruled over by a Sunni monarchy. There had been sporadic protests at various times over the years, but this time it would be connected to an apparently unstoppable international movement which would surely sweep away the old order and change things forever.

That, at least is what the protesters hoped and so it was that on St Valentine's Day, 14th February, 2011, dubbed the 'Day of Rage', the Arab Spring arrived in Bahrain. A huge march, culminating in a rally at the Pearl Roundabout, a mere stone's throw from my apartment, was carefully watched over by the police, but was nevertheless allowed to proceed. The authorities no doubt hoped that having made their point, the crowds would disperse and things would return to normal. The demonstrators however had other ideas, rather than return to their homes, they set about erecting a makeshift camp at the roundabout, one of the busiest road intersections in the greater Manama area. As the days went by, more tents and other temporary structures were built, street restaurants were constructed and each day another march would culminate in a rally at the roundabout. The protesters weren't going anywhere.

In the centre of the roundabout was a large concrete structure with four enormous arms curving upwards to join at the top and supporting a round ball - a stylised pearl, or *lulu* in Arabic. The pearl was a symbol of the original wealth of the island before the discovery of oil. Pearl diving in what were then pristine waters of the Gulf was one of the main forms of employment for hundreds of Bahrainis. The monument was built to adorn an otherwise unremarkable traffic intersection and in homage to a traditional way of life. It would shortly however become the symbol of the protest movement.

During that first week of protests, I went into work each day not quite sure whether the roads to the causeway would be open. Random barricades were being set up by the protesters at various locations throughout the island and you might be allowed through, but then again you might not. Passions were running high and although this was purely a domestic dispute, I was always guided by the principle of not wanting to be in the wrong place at the wrong time.

Having said that, I had found over the years, that all Bahrainis regardless of creed or station in life, were unfailingly friendly and welcoming towards the expatriate community. As this was an issue in which they were seeking international support, the last thing they wanted was any adverse publicity that might arise if any expatriates were targeted or harmed. I was also concerned about my daughter who had come out to Bahrain the previous year and was working as a journalist. While I was in Saudi Arabia, she was still in Bahrain and neither of us were ever quite sure whether we would be able to get home each evening.

A series of sporadic incidents occurred over the next few days which led to some fatalities. Heavily armed police manned their own road blocks across the island and the government was clearly on edge. Meanwhile the protesters continued with their marches and their sit-in at the Pearl Roundabout. I had returned home from work at the end of the working week on the Wednesday after five days of protests.

Neither my daughter, nor I had made any plans to go anywhere due to the ongoing disturbances, so we had a quiet night in the apartment, a mere five-hundred yards from the epicentre of the demonstration. From the balcony on the tenth floor of my apartment, police helicopters could be seen constantly circling the area, while on the ground below, there seemed to be an increased presence of armoured police vehicles. Something was clearly afoot.

I went down to the front entrance of the building at street level to see what was happening on the main highway. A line of armoured cars were parked immediately in front, but were not moving. Tiredness at last got the better of my curiosity and I retired to bed around eleven to be awoken around four in the morning by the sound of the helicopters and rounds of small arms fire. I went out to the balcony, but soon retreated as the scent of tear gas filled my nostrils.

Sleep would now be impossible, so I made myself a cup of coffee and turned on the television news. The Arabic Bahrain television station was obviously making an update on the situation, but their English language station was merely showing an old American sit-com. None of the international news channels were carrying anything new, so I flipped open my laptop and looked at the BBC world news website. The piece was some hours old and did not mention any unusual activity, but at the end it asked the question 'Are you there?'

On a whim, I sent a message through the link, stating who I was, where I was and my mobile phone number. About ten minutes later my phone rang. It was a production assistant from BBC in London who asked me a few questions regarding what I had seen and asked whether I was prepared to do a live World Service interview on my mobile phone. I replied that I was and they said that the presenter would call me back within a few minutes. The call came through and I was able to give a factual account of what I had seen and what was continuing to happen outside my apartment as dawn was beginning to break. The interview lasted about three minutes, but it was only when the call ended, that it dawned on me that I had been speaking to perhaps hundreds of thousands of people around the world.

The overnight events meant that the roundabout had been cleared, but the protests were far from over and there continued to be frequent violent clashes with the security forces at various locations around the island. There seemed to be a split within the senior members of the royal family regarding what measures should now be taken.

Prince Khalifa, who was the prime minister and the king's uncle, was seen as a hardliner and it appeared that the decision to violently clear the roundabout had been in line with his advice to the king. Crown Prince Salman, the king's eldest son and keen to be seen as a moderniser, had a different philosophy and he had advised that the best way to quell the disturbances was to offer the protesters some concessions and enter into a dialogue with the various opposition groups.

The Crown Prince clearly now had the king's ear, because within a few days the roundabout had once again been occupied by the protesters. There had been little opposition and the police had basically run away. Emboldened by their apparent victory, the protesters started to erect semi-permanent structures at the roundabout including a stage with a sound system from which the crowds could be addressed. Numerous stalls were set up selling revolutionary merchandise - T shirts, flags, banners and the like and there were vendors selling drinks and hot food. Every conceivable space was bedecked in flags and placards, many of which were in English for the benefit of the world's media which by now had flocked to the island to cover the unfolding story.

By 21st February and almost a week after the initial protests in Bahrain, it seemed that the whole Arab world had embarked upon a collision course with the various governments throughout the region. Surely nothing would ever be the same again. With every day that passed and crowds remaining at the roundabout, it seemed that victory would fall into their hands. Possessing few if any weapons, their defence relied upon sheer weight of numbers and to demonstrate this, the marches and demonstrations got larger and noisier every day.

The GCC leaders met in session. The other Gulf states had predominantly Sunni populations and although they were absolute monarchies, they were generally run by benevolent despots whose great oil wealth and relatively small populations, allowed them to pamper their citizens with a gold-plated welfare state. There was thus little appetite for any change in those countries, but Bahrain was the exception. It alone had a Shia majority population, had little oil wealth and in the super wealthy environment of the Gulf, it was a pauper.

Geopolitical concerns that the Arabs had about Iran and the fact that a long established monarchy was under threat, prompted the GCC to condemn the demonstrations. The Bahrain government was put on notice to resolve the problem forthwith otherwise their 'friendly neighbours' would be obliged to 'come to their assistance'.

Saudi Arabia was naturally the big player in the GCC and crucially was also home to a significant Shia population in the Eastern Province. Though sizeable, they represented only a small percentage of the overall Saudi population. Nevertheless the Saudi government had concerns that a successful uprising by the Shia in Bahrain might provoke similar problems closer to home and they were determined that under no circumstances would this be allowed to happen.

The international media were here in force and daily news broadcasts were beamed around the world live from the Pearl Roundabout with images of the protesters holding their rallies. I think it was at this point in my life when I first realised that I should not necessarily believe all the reports I saw on television, or read in the newspapers. I had lived in the country for five years and could see that the international journalists knew almost nothing about the country and what was worse, often didn't take the time to find out. The BBC in particular were guilty of this, their lead reporter daily referring to the Pearl Roundabout as Pearl Square, presumably a reference to the events that were taking place concurrently in Cairo's Tahrir Square. No-one in Bahrain recognised the term.

Another major failing of the media was the over-simplification of the struggle. It was characterised as a wicked tyrant king oppressing his people who wanted nothing more than an end to human rights abuses and democratic freedoms. Most expatriates in Bahrain knew very well that the situation was far more nuanced. Naturally the protesters hoping to gain international support, portrayed the uprising in just this way and the media largely bought it without question.

There was of course an element of striving for democracy in all this, but religion in my opinion played at least an equal, if not greater part. The opposition leaders were almost without exception, Shia clerics who in both appearance and words, bore a far greater resemblance to their co-religionists in Iran than to any progressive democratic advocates.

The BBC and other media completely failed to take this into account either through ignorance, or because of a political agenda of their own, or as I would call it - International News for the Under 5s. Many of my fellow British expatriates in Bahrain, some who had lived there for decades and had a genuine love for the country, were similarly appalled at the misrepresentation of the situation by the various media organisations.

Anyway, enough of politics. The GCC talks continued and from various statements and press releases, it was clear to see which way the wind was blowing. The protesters were living on borrowed time, though they remained defiant and the encampment at the roundabout continued to grow in size. Every day marches and rallies would take place, especially on Fridays when some marches involved nearly a million people.

I witnessed the largest of these when it passed along the highway and outside the front door of my apartment block. It took more than two hours for the people to file past, twenty abreast. The women dressed in black formed separate sections from the men and everywhere, the red and white Bahraini flag was evident. The people taking part were neither violent, or aggressive and did not mind me taking photos, or filming them.

Throughout this time, I continued to drive across the causeway to work every day and my daughter continued to go into the offices of the Bahrain Tribune, albeit by a circuitous route to avoid the Pearl Roundabout which was naturally closed to traffic. The days passed with sporadic incidents taking place across the island, sometimes met with force by the authorities and sometimes not. There were also a series of significant counter demonstrations held by hundreds of thousands of Bahrainis who remained loyal to the King and were quite content to maintain the status quo. These loyalist demonstrations were given scant coverage by much of the western media.

The causeway had remained open throughout this period, but was effectively only being used by expat commuters like myself. The Saudis - both Sunni and Shia, having seen the coverage on television, were too frightened to visit. One of our work vessels was under repair at the Bahrain Shipbuilding and Repair Company (BASREC) at Mina Sulman. The Filipino crew had remained on board while the work was carried out as they had sailed the vessel down to Bahrain from Saudi waters and due to visa restrictions were not allowed to disembark. They received a portion of their wages in cash and this would normally have been taken over to them by one of the Saudi payroll employees, but due to the ongoing unrest, they were reluctant to make the trip. As I was travelling back and forth every day, I agreed to do the payroll run on their behalf and so went down to the port and boarded the vessel which was tied up at one of the piers.

The crew were naturally pleased to see me, not only because I had brought a briefcase full of cash, but because they had been feeling a bit isolated due to the current situation in Bahrain. I assured them, as much as one could, that as they were tied up in Mina Sulman, a military facility, they were probably in one of the safest locations anywhere in Bahrain.

This point was illustrated by the fact that a number of US naval vessels shared the pier with our vessel and security was likely to be tight. After a mug of tea and half an hour or so of chat, I left the vessel and began the long walk back along the pier in the gathering nightfall, towards the dock entrance. I suddenly came face to face with an enormous and heavily armed US soldier barring my way. 'Can I help you sir?' he asked politely.

'It's OK' I replied, 'I've just been visiting one of my company's vessels. I showed him my identity card before he asked for it and after a brief examination, he wished me a pleasant evening before waving me on my way.

One evening later that week as I left the causeway on the Bahrain side, I found that many of the roads I would normally take to reach my apartment were blocked, either by the police or by protesters. I called my daughter who had also been unable to get back to the apartment. By a circuitous route we managed to rendezvous at the Dilmun Club in Saar. I was able to get in touch with a Canadian colleague who lived nearby and my daughter and I were able to spend the night at his villa. The following day we went to our respective places of work and in the evening were both able to get home. It played on my mind however, that this was an unpredictable situation which could rapidly spiral out of control.

The days passed in an uneasy stand-off. I would sometimes take a walk down to the pearl roundabout in the evenings, just ten minutes away. The place was en fête, flags and banners festooned the pearl monument and were emblazoned across the many stalls. The media were still there in force, reporters doing pieces to camera and television crews were everywhere. The demonstrators were friendly and anxious to display their yearning for democracy and freedom.

I had been on the phone to my wife who was in the UK, but who was planning to fly out in just a few days' time. She had seen the television footage of the demonstrations, but decided that a mere local disturbance should not prevent her from making the visit and she arrived on 10th March. During the next couple of days, the disturbances throughout the island increased and in some of confrontations, the police and army had been forced to retreat. I advised my daughter not to go into work and for them both to stay in the apartment, at least while I was away at work on the other side of the causeway in Saudi Arabia.

On Sunday, 13th March the police moved to clear the protesters from the financial district about a mile from the Pearl Roundabout. There were violent clashes with the use of tear gas and rubber bullets. The protesters were moved from that particular location, but the demonstrations continued. I drove into work as usual the following morning, the scent of tear gas heavy in the air. At the end of the road a handful of protesters had dragged the trunk of a palm tree across the road, but they pulled it away as I approached. I gave them a friendly wave and thumbs up as I drove past and proceeded to the causeway.

The situation remained tense and I made numerous phone calls to my wife throughout the day to make sure all was well. I heard on the news that the Bahrain government had formally asked Saudi Arabia and the UAE to provide military assistance to deal with the insurrection and that this request had been acted upon. Both countries sent hundreds of armoured vehicles and thousands of personnel across the causeway while I was at work. I decided that this would be my last day in the office and met with the CEO in the afternoon to tell him that I would be staying at home for the next couple of days. He understood the situation and told me to take care.

I returned home that evening across an eerily deserted causeway. It was clear that things were about to turn ugly and that I needed to be at home with my family and not stranded in Saudi Arabia unable to reach them. We did not venture out that evening and the following day, the king announced a state of emergency with a dusk to dawn curfew. Still the protests continued, but whereas before there had existed a state of celebratory euphoria, now there was just an aura of tense foreboding. They had seen the tanks and armoured vehicles crossing the causeway and knew that time was running out on the weeks of marches and protests.

That evening, I went down to the ground floor lobby to have a word with the concierge and his staff who all appeared nervous. I found some of the other residents already there, discussing the latest situation and some of the security options. The staff had already locked and bolted the main front doors, but there was an underground car park with an entrance and exit ramp for vehicles together with a lift and staircase to access the floors above. We were concerned that in the probable flight from the roundabout, some protestors might try to get into the building to escape from the police.

The underground car park was a potential weak point. Five of us went out of the rear door and down into the car park. We then blockaded the vehicle ramp with a couple of cars which were parked as closely together as possible. We then barricaded the doors which led to the lift and rear staircase with heavy tables which had been stored in an underground room. A collection of chairs was piled on top. This would at least block any opportunist access from the car park.

We spent the remainder of that evening alternating between watching the news on various international television stations and looking out of the windows to see what was happening on the ground below. It was eerily quiet and so we decided on an early night, at least we would be able to sleep reasonably well knowing that we had made it extremely difficult for anyone to enter the building.

Chapter 33

Spring is Over

At dawn the following morning, I became aware of the persistent thump of helicopter rotor blades. I swiftly got out of bed and went out on to the balcony. In the half light, I could see two army helicopter gunships circling overhead, a couple of hundred feet above me. Off to my left in the direction of the Pearl Roundabout, smoke was billowing from something evidently on fire, the smoke mingling with clouds of tear gas, while the sound of small arms fire came on the soft morning breeze.

The government had clearly made their move and the long awaited operation was well underway. I switched on the television news to get an update on events. It was strange to watch live television footage of events which were happening just a few hundred yards away.

The helicopters were clearly there to intimidate the protesters rather than to fire upon them and I never saw them opening fire at any time. I went out onto the balcony several times and could see the helicopters hovering almost at the same height as my apartment. I thought it best to come inside lest they might think I was a protester about to take a potshot at them.

By late morning the action seemed to be over, the helicopters had departed and the clouds of smoke had gradually drifted away, only the faint, distinctive scent of tear gas still permeated the air. It turned out that many of the protesters had crept away from the roundabout during the small hours of the night. The army were left to clear a relatively small number of individuals who had set light to the temporary structures as they retreated.

The government were going to make sure that this time, there would be no repeat of the events a month earlier when having cleared the demonstrators, they allowed them to re-assemble once again. Over the following days, widespread arrests took place of many prominent activists together with those who had been caught engaging in acts of violence.

The government announced that a state of emergency and dusk to dawn curfews would remain in place until further notice. The tension was palpable and we didn't feel that it was altogether safe to leave our apartment for the time being. We spent the time alternating between watching news broadcasts on television and observing the scene outside. The roads remained empty and all was eerily quiet.

After twenty four hours of being confined in the apartment, I ventured down to the pool to have swim. The pool was located at one side of the apartment block, above the vehicle entrance to the car park. I noticed that on the bottom of the pool were a number of small, black objects, so I jumped in and swam down to investigate. I retrieved a couple of the objects and on reaching the surface, discovered that they were discharged rubber bullets. It was difficult to determine whether they were from the night before, or from one of the disturbances during previous days. I kept them, thinking that they would make interesting souvenirs of these strange days.

During the tumultuous events of the past weeks, shops, restaurants and other businesses had largely remained open. Now, with the state of emergency and dusk to dawn curfews, many shops were closed. A brief survey of the contents of our refrigerator revealed that we had very little food. This might be a problem.

My wife gathered together the few tins of food - beans, peas etc. and a few other items and planned some not very appetising meals for the next few days. In all our concerns about safety, we hadn't thought to stock up on food. The question was, how long would the stores remain closed and when would it be safe to venture out?

It was now Wednesday, two days before the weekend. Shops and supermarkets, especially those selling food, normally remained open seven days a week, but it seemed that the whole of Bahrain was in collective shock. The Shia had fled back to their villages, frightened for their lives and property, while the Sunni and the large expatriate population were left in a state of limbo.

I could see that the roads around the apartment building were still deserted and it looked like we would be staying home again that evening. I waited with bated breath to see what culinary delights my wife might be making from our meagre supplies. It was to be ......beans on toast. Fortunately I had been to the bottle store a week or so earlier and had an adequate supply of beer and wine so all was not lost. Hopefully the shops would re-open soon.

The following morning I took a solo reconnaissance drive to see what was happening beyond the immediate vicinity of the apartment. There were a few cars on the roads, but not many. The Pearl Roundabout was still encircled by rows of armoured vehicles and you couldn't get close, but the roads in the opposite direction were open. I drove past quite a few stores which were closed, until I found a small supermarket on the Budaiya Highway which was open. It wasn't a shop I had ever been into before and the food on sale seemed to be more geared to the local market - rice, vegetables etc. I managed to fill a basket with some basic essentials and returned home. It might not be enough for a feast, but at least it would be an improvement on beans on toast!

We stayed in the apartment for the remainder of the day and in the evening, together with some of the other residents, dismantled the improvised barricade we had hastily erected in the basement. Tomorrow was Friday and it was announced that curfew restrictions would be marginally relaxed until six in the evening.

We went for a drive and found that most shops, supermarkets, restaurants and hotels had re-opened. It was time to get a drink, the only snag being that I had received a call from a friend who needed a lift to the airport later that day as taxis had temporarily disappeared from the streets.

That afternoon we drove to the Ritz-Carlton hotel and headed into Trader Vic's for a drink with some friends who had also heard that the bar - one of my favourite watering holes - was open. It was most definitely the time for some celebratory cocktails. I had one drink and then, leaving my wife with our friends, picked up my colleague from his villa and drove him to the airport.

He was running late, so I waited for him for fifteen minutes and then left for the airport. As we crossed the flyover which ran past the Pearl Roundabout, I could see some heavy construction equipment. The government were clearly wasting no time in demolishing the concrete monument which had come to symbolise the uprising.

I dropped him off and headed back to the Ritz-Carlton. All was well until I pulled off the highway onto the exit ramp which would take me back to the hotel and found my way blocked by an armoured vehicle. The soldiers at either side signalled for me to stop and I lowered the window. The curfew had started ten minutes ago he said. Damn! I had quite forgotten.

I apologised, turned the car around and manoeuvred the car over some open ground to park near my apartment. I wondered how on earth I was going to get back to my wife at the hotel, if indeed I could get back at all. It was obvious that I couldn't get there by car as all the roads were be blocked by military or police vehicles.

Unable to contact anyone at the Ritz-Carlton by phone, I set off on foot, heading towards the main intersection beneath the highway flyover which was the only realistic way of getting to the hotel. It was still light, but it was now half an hour past the curfew hour of six o'clock. As I approached the intersection, I could see a collection of army vehicles and some groups of soldiers. I decided that the best course of action was to walk slowly towards them and rely on the fact that I didn't look like a local and therefore presented no threat.

I waved and sort of minced towards them hoping that I represented the very opposite of an aggressive, masculine appearance. As I got closer, I could see the heavy machine gun mounted on one of the armoured vehicles cranking round to point in my direction and I once again waved. Hoping that their orders didn't include 'shoot on sight' and half expecting a rattle of fire at any moment, I at last reached the soldiers with my hands held aloft.

'I have a bit of a problem,' I announced. I had forgotten about the curfew and need to collect my wife from the Ritz Carlton and take her home. The soldier evidently understood English and motioned to another group of what appeared to be officers. One of them came over. I could see from his epaulets that he was a major and when he spoke to me his English was impeccable, possibly a Sandhurst graduate. I explained the situation to him and he instructed me to continue on foot to the hotel. I should then collect my wife, return to the road block and report to him. I set off towards the hotel and ten minutes later I was back inside Trader Vic's. I explained to my wife and other friends that they had better make a move as we were in breach of the curfew. We grabbed a ride with one of our friends who lived out at Saar and he drove slowly back towards the army roadblock.

He pulled up and we got out. The officer I had spoken with earlier was still there. He instructed the driver to proceed to Saar which was further out of town as there were no further roadblocks in that direction. My apartment however was back towards the city. 'It is too dangerous to go there on your own.' the officer said. 'We will escort you.' We walked with him to an Army Land Rover and my wife and I climbed into the back. He got in front with the driver and motioned for a group of four soldiers to follow in an armoured vehicle.

We reached my apartment five minutes later and when we pulled up outside, the four soldiers jumped out of the following vehicle and set up a defensive perimeter around us, crouching down in the road with automatic rifles at the ready, pointing in all four directions. We then got out of the Land Rover and headed up the steps into the main entrance of the apartment block, the officer giving us a smart salute as we disappeared inside.

I laughed when we got inside and said to my wife that I had been a bit worse for wear on some previous visits to Trader Vic's, but I had never required an armed military escort to get me home. I suppose there's a first time for everything.

The state of emergency lasted for two weeks. The concrete monument at the Pearl Roundabout was completely demolished and the whole area was sealed off to both motor and pedestrian traffic. No marches, or other protests were allowed anywhere and at any time throughout the island. The protesters were now back in their villages which were scattered across the island and although there continued to be some riots and disturbances, these were contained in the villages and never allowed to spill out onto any main roads. I learned later that this is a crowd control procedure called 'kettling'. The only people who suffered disruption to their daily lives, or damage to their property, were the residents of the villages themselves.

A few days later I read a report about Bahrain on the BBC news website regarding the aftermath of the uprising. There were reports of arbitrary arrests, the rounding up of various opposition leaders as well as reports of torture and other human rights abuses. While I have no doubt that some of these were true, I and many other expatriates had been frustrated by the BBC and other news organisations which many of us considered not to have been even-handed throughout the past months and had largely ignored the religious element to the conflict.

I clicked on the 'Are you there? - What have you seen?' link at the end of the piece as I had done previously. Sure enough the call came through on my mobile and the editorial assistant asked me some routine questions. In my answers I mentioned that I had already given a live interview to the World Service earlier on in the disturbances. She asked me what I had to say and I mentioned that I felt that their reports lacked a little even-handedness and although there were undoubtedly some human rights abuses, Bahrain was basically a liberal country where all faiths could worship openly. It was a place which was open to people and commerce from around the world.

It also hosted British and American military bases which helped keep the gulf shipping lanes open and deter Iranian threats to western oil supplies. Above all, I said they had failed to adequately explain the religious element in the uprising, which had it been successful, would in my opinion, have led to an Islamic theocracy, the end of free religious practice and the death knell of what was in many respects, a largely liberal society. She said that she would speak to the producer and call me back. I'm still waiting for the call.

The protests continued and still continue to this day, to mark certain anniversaries, but they rarely impact any areas outside of the Shia villages and are never allowed to approach the city centre, or any public areas. Protesters, usually teenagers, will often block minor roads with makeshift barricades of burning tyres, but they are just a minor irritation to drivers. Then as now, none of this violence, anger and frustration has to my knowledge, ever boiled over into attacks on the expatriate population.

Things superficially returned to normal, but something had

changed. The discontent and anger hadn't gone away, it had merely been bottled up. Perhaps Bahrain will never again be the placid and fun loving place it had been, or maybe that had only ever existed in my imagination.

Chapter 34

New Boss and New Apartment

Life continued and work was increasingly occupying my waking hours. The situation with the banks had not improved and with things grinding to a standstill, the 'new broom' CEO had been abruptly relieved of his duties. His replacement was a young Scotsman who, rather than having a background in construction, had a background in finance. It was a sign that any future business activity would be related to managing the mountain of debt and the disposal of assets rather than in pursuing new construction business.

The new CEO and I hit it off right away. I could see that as far as he was concerned, the financial rescue of the company was paramount and that this might require some painful sacrifices. It was also true that we were still working on multiple projects with an order book worth almost a billion dollars. He brought in some of his own people and despatched the few remaining Saudi executives within the first two weeks of his tenure. He realised that I might be useful to him chiefly because of my experience and my contacts within Aramco, still one of our major clients, and he promoted me to the position of Vice-President - Commercial.

With the banks retaining an iron grip on our bank accounts,

it was clearly going to be something of a tightrope walk to continue our multiple operations and make the huge payments to the workforce and sub-contractors. If that wasn't going to be difficult enough, the Saudi Stock Market Authority (CMA) announced that they would be conducting an investigation into the initial flotation which took place back in 2008. Fun times!

A year after the Bahrain uprising, the lease expired on my apartment at Al Jazeera. Although the apartment was convenient, spacious and had great views towards the south of the island, it seemed a little tired, or maybe I had tired of it. I had been there for more than three years and I felt that I needed a change. My daughter had been living with me for the past two years and so we began to look at alternative options.

A complex of three, ultra-modern towers called *Abraaj al Lulu* (Pearl Towers) had been built adjacent to the Pearl Roundabout in 2009. It was one of the most luxurious apartment complexes in Bahrain, containing indoor and outdoor swimming pools, tennis courts, squash courts and cinemas. As might be imagined, this came at a high price, but things had changed. Scarred by their proximity to the former centre of unrest during the Bahrain uprising, they could now be accessed only by passing through a military checkpoint. The barbed wire perimeter which had been thrown around the roundabout also encircled the apartment complex. The net result of all this was that rental prices had plummeted. A three bedroomed apartment in the most prestigious Black Tower had formerly commanded a monthly rent of around three thousand dollars, but could now be rented for the equivalent of two thousand. It seemed too good to be true,

I went to look at an apartment in the Black Tower and met

the owner, a lovely lady who was a member of a renowned Bahraini merchant family. The apartment was impeccably furnished and had amazing views to the sea on one side and along the corniche from the other. The facilities were second to none and better yet, the monthly rental was almost half what it had been prior to the uprising. The only downside was that entering the complex necessitated passing through an army checkpoint, but this could hardly be considered onerous, particularly in this part of the world. I also reasoned that it was probably one of the safest places on the island, after all who, other than heads of state and government officials, have their residences guarded by the army around the clock. And so, early in 2012, I moved into the Black Tower at *Abraaj al Lulu*.

I would occasionally go jogging in the evenings, but as I often returned from work late and hungry, I generally exercised only at weekends. The *Abraaj Al Lulu* complex was surrounded by quite a few acres of undeveloped land. I would usually head out through the military checkpoint and then take a route in one of many directions away from the apartment.

The slip road leading off the main highway in front of the apartment complex led to the now closed Pearl Roundabout, blocked off by a manned military checkpoint. Just for the hell of it, I decided one day to double back and head along the footpath which ran alongside the slip road.

As I approached the checkpoint, a Bahraini soldier came towards me and indicated that I should stop. I asked him whether it would be all right to complete my run further down the road towards the roundabout. He replied that it was not allowed and when I asked him why, he replied 'Because it is too dangerous.' I laughed and said, 'But there is no-one there, how can it be dangerous?' He smiled and said that it was dangerous to go down there because if I did, he would have to shoot me!

Needless to say, I turned around and headed back the way I came. At least the man had a sense of humour.

At work, I increasingly spent more time talking to bankers than to clients, but occasionally I would still have to visit some of our ongoing projects. We had been working on a new refinery for Aramco in Yanbu. Part of the project involved the construction of a flare stack which would be the tallest one in the Western Province of Saudi Arabia. A huge gleaming metal structure, it had been painstakingly fabricated on the ground and then hoisted up, one section at a time and affixed to the previously erected ones. When complete it towered more than four hundred feet above the desert.

Aramco always liked to hold a celebration to commemorate various project milestones and this was one of them. The CEO was invited to attend the celebration and receive a token of appreciation from the client for the efforts of our workforce in achieving this historic goal. Two days before the planned ceremony the CEO informed me that due to a domestic emergency, he had to return to the UK and that I would have to represent the company at the celebration in Yanbu.

I flew over and arrived at Aramco's offices in the grounds of which, was a huge marquee. This was the venue for the celebratory lunch and speeches. About five-hundred employees and senior managers of Aramco were in attendance. I was asked to say a few words of appreciation to the combined efforts of both our own and the Aramco workforce. After the speeches were finished, I was presented with a framed, metal plaque which in addition to carrying an engraved picture of the aforementioned flare stack, bore the legend; *'The Largest Erection in the Western Province'*. Absolutely priceless!

I was hoping to keep the plaque in my own office - possibly forever, but when the CEO returned to work and read the immortal inscription, he insisted that it belonged in his office and it was thereafter displayed in a prominent position on his desk.

It was around this time that my daughter decided that Bahrain was just a little too sleepy and that she would like to relocate to Dubai as a number of her friends and acquaintances had done over the preceding few months. She flew out in May 2013 after living with me for almost four years. I had got used to having her around and it was a sad day when she left. Little did I know that a mere three months later I would be joining her in the UAE.

Chapter 35

Life in The Emirates

In September 2013, the CEO invited me up to his office to discuss the new slimmed down management structure required to take the company forward and avoid financial collapse. The new organisation chart had been in circulation among executive managers for a couple of days and I had noted that my position had disappeared. This was hardly surprising considering that we were no longer able to bid for new projects, but I decided to wait and see when we might have this conversation. To be perfectly honest I wasn't unduly concerned. I had already turned sixty-one and didn't wish to continue working forever. I was however intrigued at what the CEO might say.

'Ah Stuart' he said as I came in. 'You will have seen the new organisation chart?' I replied that I had. 'You're not on it,' he said with a smile.

'I had noticed that.' I replied. 'I was wondering when you were going to enlighten me.' He laughed. We both knew that the chances of the company surviving in its present form were looking increasingly slim and if it did, it would certainly not be undertaking any new projects or signing any contracts in the near future. He then said, 'You have been a great help to me over the past twelve months and I really appreciate the support you've given me. Although your position isn't on the new chart, I do have another a job for you.' The job he had in mind would however not be in Saudi Arabia, but in Abu Dhabi.

Almost four years earlier the company had established a joint venture with a state holding company in Abu Dhabi. Though it was a very small start-up construction company, the idea was to take advantage of the many projects currently underway in the UAE as a result of sky-high oil prices. The plan was to use our construction expertise, while the holding company would provide fifty one percent of the capital equity and utilise its high-level political and commercial connections within the Emirates to obtain contracts.

The general manager of the joint venture was appointed by the Saudi Arabian partner while the chairman and finance director were appointees of the holding company. The firm had rolled along for the past few years with a couple of fairly small projects, but hadn't really taken off in the way that either of the partners had envisaged when the company was founded. I suspect that this had as much to do with a lack of investment rather than for any reasons of poor management. Neither party it seemed, was willing to invest more in the enterprise than they already had.

To add to the problem, the existing general manager had fallen out with the both the chairman and another director and they were demanding action to replace him. The CEO wished to comply with their demands and in view of the Saudi company's parlous position, basically wanted to shut the operation down without creating any ill will with the partner company in Abu Dhabi. In short, this would be a hatchet job without appearing to be one. I flew down to Abu Dhabi and met with the chairman and finance director.

I had told my CEO that I was contemplating retirement in the not too distant future, but promised him that I would do the job for a year, or until the company was wound up, whichever came first. I did not share this with the joint venture chairman and managed to get on quite well with him. He was an Iraqi and had an interesting background, having been deputy oil minister in the government of Saddam Hussein prior to the 2003 invasion of Iraq. Educated in the UK, he was very old school and a gentleman, though I had been warned that I should never completely trust him.

I left Saudi Arabia in October 2013 and surrendered my residency. This would be my final farewell to a country that I had called home for almost twenty five years. I gave two months' notice to my landlady in Bahrain indicating that I would be vacating the apartment and prepared to move to the United Arab Emirates. There would be sufficient time to visit my friends in Aramco's Dhahran community and to make a final visit to the places which held so many memories. I knew that I would never return.

I found it amazing just how many possessions I had managed to accumulate in a short space of time. I had only lived in Bahrain for eight years and in all that time had resided in fully furnished apartments, yet I had to organise a shipment of personal effects far larger than it really should have been. Clothing, bedding, rugs, bikes and so on. Fortunately, the shipping company informed me that they could make the shipment overland via the causeway, through Saudi Arabia and down to the Emirates rather than the more expensive option of an air shipment.

My temporary home would be the Beach Rotana Hotel in Abu Dhabi. It was a nice hotel and as the name suggests, had its own private beach on one of the inlets which surround the 'island' of Abu Dhabi, an arrow shaped peninsula bordered by multiple shallow inlets of the sea. I had been assigned a driver, Stanley Nixon, who despite his English sounding name, hailed from Kerala in India. He was a lovely man. The hotel was only a ten minute drive from the office and so every morning after breakfast, I would walk out of the hotel to my waiting car and Stanley would drive me to the office.

It may sound like a life of luxury and luxurious it certainly was, but living in a hotel, even a five star one, begins to pale after a while. I knew that the company would not continue to pay my hotel bills indefinitely and that before long, I would need to rent a place of my own. I had a word with my government affairs man, a Syrian who had lived in Abu Dhabi for more than ten years and had a great many contacts. He came up with a few suggestions and I viewed some of the apartments. All were nice and would have been adequate, though I was conscious that my tenure in this place was not going to be long-term and had no intention of signing a lease longer than one year.

My daughter was living up in Dubai, a one hour drive north of Abu Dhabi and sharing an apartment with some friends while she looked for a job. I had spent the last eight years commuting across from Bahrain to Saudi Arabia and wasn't keen to once again spend several hours a day on the road. Nevertheless, Dubai and Abu Dhabi are very different places, each pleasant in its own way, but there are huge contrasts. Abu Dhabi was the capital of the UAE and had virtually all of the oil wealth. It was a quieter, well laid out business city, but unexciting. Dubai on the other hand was the freewheeling capital of entertainment and excess. It was home to the biggest, longest, highest and fastest of seemingly everything.

A major tourist destination, it had a multitude of entertainment venues, golf courses, bars, restaurants and hotels even an indoor ski slope! More importantly, it had a huge number of apartments and villas for rent at rates which were somewhat lower than Abu Dhabi. The distance from Dubai to Abu Dhabi was around seventy miles, but the eight lane highway connecting the two cities was fast, with no annoying and time consuming passport and customs checks. I reckoned I could commute to my office in an hour and fifteen minutes.

Living in Dubai meant that I could share an apartment with my daughter and not have to continue subsidising her rental payments. The more I thought about it, the more it made sense. I mentioned my search for accommodation one day to the project manager and he said that he knew a Dutch couple who had an apartment in Dubai which they were prepared to rent out for a few months as they were returning to Europe. It would be somewhere to live until I found something more permanent. I went to meet them and had a look at their beautiful apartment in *Al Fattan Towers* right on Jumeirah Beach Road - one of the most desirable locations in Dubai. We agreed a price for a three-month rent and my daughter and I moved in the following week.

The drive to Abu Dhabi each day proved fairly easy and I was able to drive as fast as conditions would allow, but of course, the local drivers were always faster. It seemed strange living in what was essentially a tourist beach resort and leaving for work each day, just as holidaymakers were heading to the beach.

Work was a challenge. It seemed that my predecessor had been happy to let things tick over without trying too hard to obtain any additional business. The company called itself a construction outfit, but had virtually no assets to speak of. Few vehicles, no heavy equipment and more than half of the labour force was rented from manpower supply companies. It was in short, a company going nowhere. It had three current projects, a small one with Hyundai at the oil centre of Ruwais which had apparently stalled for many months, a fuel pipeline within a naval base currently under construction plus a small part of the construction of a palace for the King of Bahrain who had recently married a member of the Dubai ruling family.

I calculated that with a bit of careful planning and a lot of luck, we could complete all three by the end of the following year. The Saudi company could then make an orderly retreat without ruffling too many feathers in the UAE and I could retire. Job done, or at least that's what I thought.

A few months prior to my arrival, a team of estimators had been sent down to Abu Dhabi from Dammam to help the joint venture with the bidding on new projects. The idea was to utilise experienced staff normally based in Saudi Arabia who were no longer bidding for any new work. Although the Saudi company wanted to close down the operation, they wished to appear pro-active to the joint venture partner. They had been diligently working away and bids for a number of projects had been submitted. Incredibly, within a month of my arrival, we had been awarded five new contracts including some with the biggest player in town, the Abu Dhabi National Oil Company (ADNOC).

Timing, as they say, is everything. The chairman was over the moon that after limping along for the past few years, the company was at last being awarded new contracts and he would be able to give the main board some good news. My role in obtaining this new business was minimal to say the least, but they clearly seemed to think that I was somehow responsible for this miraculous turnaround in company fortunes and to be honest, I didn't try too hard to persuade them otherwise.

And so, rather than winding the company down, I would now have to expand operations. I would need to hire additional manpower and spend money the company didn't have on buying or renting equipment and signing multiple contracts for the supply of services and materials. I was certainly going to be busy.

I had the nagging doubt however, that the team of estimators had not fully understood the local market when they formulated the bids. My more pressing concern was knowing that the precarious financial position of the Saudi partner meant I would have little, or no working capital with which to perform this new work. It was quite a different scenario to the one I had in mind when agreeing to take on the job.

The apartment in *Al Fattan Towers* was fine for the time being, but it now looked as though I might be in the UAE for a little longer than originally envisioned. My daughter and I began to look for somewhere more permanent and the choice as you can imagine, was endless. Dubai must be the ultimate transient city in the world and although it had a number of long-term resident expatriates, like many other places in the Gulf, most were working there on a short term basis. One thing was for sure, I would be able to find something suitable without too much difficulty.

Dubai had sprawled along the coast from its origins as a tiny mud-brick collection of buildings at the mouth of the Dubai Creek, to a mega city in the short space of thirty years. The skyline seemed to change on an almost daily basis, the desert sky punctuated with gleaming new high rise buildings with many others still under construction. The rule seemed to be that the next building had to be even taller, grander and more unusual than its predecessors. The demand for building land was so great, they had even reclaimed land from the sea. The Jumeirah Palm was the most famous of these, so large it could be seen from space. It was home to a variety of expensive villas and apartments as well as many plush hotels. Another two 'palms' were under construction, one at Jebel Ali and another near the mouth of Dubai creek.

Further out to sea and unconnected to the mainland, work was proceeding apace on 'The World' a representation of the world map created by sand dredged from the bottom of the sea, though quite who would wish to purchase, or build a property on any of these somewhat isolated artificial islands was anyone's guess. The philosophy in Dubai always seemed to be; 'if we build it, they will come.'

I soon got used to living in the heart of tourist Dubai. The apartment was on Jumeirah Beach Road, a stone's throw from the sandy beach and the warm, blue waters of the Gulf with the amazing Marina just behind. There were many other districts of the sprawling city state that I could look for a place to live, but I knew that I wanted to stay in this area which also had the practical benefit of being located on the Abu Dhabi side of the city with Sheikh Zayed Road, just five minutes away. Rentals were considerably more expensive in this part of Dubai than they had been in Bahrain, so I decided to downsize from three to two bedrooms and found a great apartment on the top floor of a fully serviced apartment with swimming pool, gym and underground parking barely a hundred yards away from where I had been temporarily living. As was usual in Dubai at that time, landlords demanded an entire year's rent in advance, so the deal was done and we moved in at the end of January 2014.

As I expected, once the euphoria of the new project awards had passed, I was faced with the reality of trying to expand the company on a shoestring. My time during the past two years in Saudi Arabia had prepared me for this scenario, but it was nevertheless a struggle to balance the cashflow with the need to make payments to contractors. This was particularly difficult as it was basically a subcontract operation and if bills were not paid on time, services could be immediately removed whether it be manpower, or equipment.

Our first new project was to build five motorway style service stations for ADNOC in the Abu Dhabi area. These had multiple fuel pumps, car repair facilities, fast food outlets and convenience shops. This contract award had been followed by the award of a project for the construction of a primary school, also for ADNOC, in the oil producing town of Ruwais, a hundred miles west of Abu Dhabi. The third project award, rapidly following on from the earlier ones, was for the construction of an underground nuclear bomb-proof military command bunker. If I told you that no-one in the company had the remotest idea of how to build a nuclear bomb-proof bunker, you should not be entirely surprised. I began to worry.

There was more to contract awards than merely being

competitive on price and I became aware of a local Emirati who used to visit our offices, chiefly to speak with my senior project manager, an Iraqi. They would sit for hours discussing things in Arabic and I was eventually introduced to him, his name was Mughram and although an Emirati, unusually he spoke very little English.

The project manager informed me that he was the joint venture's Mr Fixit. A childhood friend of the UAE Minister of Interior, he was sufficiently well-connected to assist in the award of new business. He had an office at the joint venture headquarters building where I occasionally bumped into him. It seemed that he had a somewhat love-hate relationship with both the chairman and the finance director. The conflict seemed to stem from the amount of bonus to which he considered he was entitled to as a result of any new contract awards, whether he had been instrumental in obtaining them, or not.

I had no intention of getting involved in the Byzantine inner workings of Emirati relationships and decided from the beginning to avoid contact as much as possible. I would leave the chairman to deal with him. This however was easier said than done and over the next few months I found myself inexorably drawn into the murky world of Emirati political and business intrigue. This was clear when I was invited for a negotiation meeting after we had submitted our aforementioned bid for a nuclear proof underground bunker for the UAE Armed Forces.

The part of the armed forces responsible for all permanent military facilities was called the Command for Military Works (CMW), the headquarters of which, was located half an hour's drive south of Abu Dhabi. The meeting would be with the brigadier-general and the chairman told me that I must take

Mughram with me as he knew the brigadier-general well. How much influence he might have over the award of the contract however, remained to be seen. I was aware of how much profit and provision for contingencies we had built into our bid for this project and it didn't leave too much 'wiggle room' in the inevitable wrangling that I knew was about to take place.

Mughram picked me up from my office half an hour late in his Bentley Continental and proceeded to drive like a madman out to the headquarters of CMW. Security was tight and we had to surrender mobile phones at the gatehouse before we were allowed in to the complex which was completely surrounded by thirty foot high concrete walls. After passing through a series of scanners and x-ray machines we then had to proceed on foot to the main administration building.

We were ushered into the brigadier-general's palatial conference room which had a connecting door to his office. Mughram insisted that he would not be getting involved in any of the technical, or commercial discussions and was only there 'to be there'. I knew exactly what he meant. After waiting for ten minutes, the door opened and in strode a small, self-important looking man in an immaculate khaki uniform, his gold-braided epaulettes probably making him look bulkier than he actually was.

He was flanked by two young Emirati lady officers dressed in camouflage fatigues, but wearing black headscarves topped with bright scarlet berets set at jaunty angles. I certainly wasn't expecting that. The brigadier-general, the lady officers and I exchanged pleasantries for a few minutes before we got down to business. I had learned over many years in Arabia that getting straight to the point is considered the height of bad manners.

One of the lady officers was exceptionally beautiful and I couldn't help, but notice that she was quite flirty. I wasn't expecting that either. Eventually, with pleasantries over, it was down to the negotiation. The brigadier general's opening gambit was to announce that the bid price was way too high and couldn't possibly be accepted. This I was expecting.

I knew that we wouldn't have been invited to this meeting had our bid not been competitive, so I calmly pointed out that we had made every attempt to keep our price as low as possible. He smiled and said that there is always room for manoeuvre. I nodded and then launched into a yarn about being a relatively small local company, eager to perform work for such a prestigious client as the UAE Armed Forces. I added that we were so anxious to obtain this contract that despite there being very little room for manoeuvre, as a gesture of goodwill, I was prepared to lower the bid price by five percent.

In true Arabian style he threw down the file he was holding and announced that I was wasting his time. He then got up and stormed out of the conference room, followed by the two lady officers. I shrugged at Mughram who said, 'I'll deal with it.' He waited a few moments before disappearing through the door into the brigadier-general's office. I sat there twiddling my thumbs, knowing that I could go no lower than a further five percent and if that upset the brigadier general then so be it.

Ten minutes later the door re-opened and everyone came back into the conference room, the brigadier-general's apparent anger had disappeared and he now looked more relaxed. As he took his seat at the head of the table, Mughram came up behind him and ruffled his hair as if he were a young child. Unbelievable.

I neither knew, nor wanted to know, exactly what had been said in the office, but I decided to reduce the offer a further five percent to try and seal the deal. If he rejected this, I would be the one walking out of the conference room. I was relieved that this gesture was greeted with warm smiles and handshakes. We had secured a new client in the shape of the UAE Armed Forces. Whether we actually knew how to build a nuclear proof bunker, or indeed whether we could make any money out of the deal, remained to be seen, but they would be problems for another day.

Plagued by cash flow constraints and the consequent inability to pay our sub-contractors on time, I became used to the sight of unpaid contractor representatives beating a path to my door every morning. I would always have tea or coffee brought to them while listening patiently to their tales of woe. I found it the best, though time consuming practice, to give them a hearing and to sympathise with their plight as I hoped they would sympathise with mine. 'I would love to pay you' I would say, but I just don't have funds at the moment. Delayed payments from some of our clients didn't help matters and I used this situation, whenever possible, to shift the blame for our financial woes onto them.

Sometimes we would receive what I called 'ransom payment' demands. This was an old ruse particularly used by contractors who were supplying items such as ready-mixed concrete, asphalt and water. They would know that we had reached a stage of construction where their product was urgently required and a precise delivery date and time would be set. An hour before the delivery was due to take place, I would receive a phone call stating that the delivery would not happen unless we first cleared their overdue payments.

This was the cue for frantic pleading and hastily arranged partial payments of the sums owed. I couldn't in all honesty blame them, but it made life difficult and put pressure on us from our clients who saw such delays as a sign of our incompetence. I could never divulge to the client the parlous state of our finances as this might lead to the cancellation of our contracts and the application of liquidated damages. This would undoubtedly send the company under and worse still, create a huge loss of face for the holding company.

Such were my challenges throughout 2014. Instead of an easy and relaxed winding down of the company, I found myself gearing up and taking on projects which to say the least, had a very uncertain outcome. Had I been ten years younger, I may have relished this challenge, but I began to find the situation endlessly frustrating and not one that I was able to remedy, if indeed it could be remedied at all.

The situation back in Saudi Arabia seemed to get worse by the day. The CEO who had asked me to move down to Abu Dhabi was summarily fired after only eighteen months in the position and replaced by another Scotsman who lived in Dubai. He called in to see me one day and seemed a pleasant enough fellow. He knew my background and was anxious to find out as much as he possibly could about the Saudi Arabian company and to a lesser extent, the small joint venture I was running in Abu Dhabi.

I felt that he had another agenda and this was revealed to me by one of the directors of the joint venture partner who said that he wanted his son to replace me. Nepotism was alive and well. Although the general manager appointment was in the hands of the Saudi partner, it still had to be approved by the Abu Dhabi board and they had refused. It wasn't all bad as he ensured that I got the bulk of my severance award from Saudi Arabia which had not been paid in full when I left.

Although my daughter was living in Dubai she hadn't yet obtained her residency permit. British nationals and most Europeans, were permitted to remain in the UAE for a period of up to a month, but were not supposed to work. Many people who were either looking for work, or working in the so-called black economy had to leave the country every month, even if only for a few hours and then re-enter for a further one-month visa to be issued. A short flight to Doha, Muscat or Bahrain was an option, but the cheapest method was to drive from Dubai to the Omani border at a place called Hatta which lay in the jagged hills of Oman.

Hatta Fort and then the village of Hatta, lay on the main road between Dubai and Muscat. At the border crossing there was an extensive complex of customs and passport controls on both the UAE and Omani side. In between Dubai and the UAE border however, there was a tiny strip of Omani territory which was a legacy of the days when these countries were British protectorates, called the Trucial States. Although fully independent for almost fifty years, the maps had never been altered to reflect modern realities. There was a UAE checkpoint on the way out and one on the way back to cover this strip of desert which was barely two miles wide. Normally this was a casual affair with just a wave or nod through.

The process at Hatta was first of all to be stamped out of the UAE then drive a mile through no man's land to the main Omani customs and passport building where an entry stamp into Oman would be issued. You would then drive back to the UAE checkpoint where the Omani stamp would be verified before receiving a new visa for a further month.

It was an hour's drive each way to Hatta and then a further hour for stamping in and out. It reminded me of the daily causeway process I endured for the previous eight years between Bahrain and Saudi Arabia though fortunately I only had to do this once a month until my daughter managed to secure a residence visa. The compensation was that the Hatta Fort Hotel did an amazing Friday brunch and on the way back there were places where dune buggies could be hired for white-knuckle rides across the sand dunes, which was always great fun.

Things didn't always go smoothly however. On one occasion we had gone through the process including waiting in a queue for half an hour in the Omani passport hall and arrived back at the UAE border point. The guard inspected my daughter's passport and announced that it contained no Omani stamp and had not therefore officially left the country. It had been a long morning and I wasn't keen on the idea of turning round and driving back to the packed passport control hall at the Omani border. I said to the guard that we had done the whole process so what would happen if we just drove on to Dubai. 'I would advise strongly against that,' he replied. 'We would have to come after you and it wouldn't end well.' Enough said.

I turned the car around and headed wearily back to Oman. When we arrived back at the hall, I jumped the queue and said to the officer behind the desk, 'We were here just half an hour ago and you forgot to put the stamp in my daughter's passport.' He remembered me, smiled and said, 'Sorry uh?' before affixing the Omani stamp. Back to the border and this time there was no problem, but I had wasted the greater part of one of my precious days off.

Aside from the frustrations of work, I was enjoying my sojourn in Dubai and found that my popularity among many friends in Saudi Arabia and the UK had increased dramatically with many requests to pay me visits. A few months later a couple of friends were visiting Dubai and we decided to meet up. I invited them for a drive into the mountains around Hatta so we could have Friday brunch at the Hatta Fort Hotel.

I picked them up from their hotel and without a care in the world headed out of town on the Hatta road. Passing through the first checkpoint with barely an acknowledgement from the guard, we drove on through the increasingly rocky landscape to the hotel. A wonderful brunch, followed by a short stroll around the gardens, then back into the car for the drive back to Dubai. It wasn't until we approached the small UAE checkpoint guarding that tiny Omani strip of desert that I realised I had neglected to ask my friends to bring their passports with them.

I was carrying my UAE residency card in my wallet which I showed to the guard in the small kiosk while explaining that I had merely taken my friends, who were both British, for lunch to Hatta Fort and that they had left their passports at the hotel in Dubai. The guard decided that any decision regarding re-entry to the UAE under these circumstances was above his pay grade. He instructed me to go and see the captain and pointed towards a small portable building, fifty yards back down the road.

I pulled over and, leaving my friends inside, went over to the building preparing to use my poor Arabic to explain that I was an idiot! How could I have forgotten about the Omani strip of land intersecting the highway? I knocked on the door and entered. The captain was fast asleep on a camp bed in the middle of the room. I coughed loudly and he sprang out of his bed looking more like a naughty schoolboy than a police captain.

After rubbing his eyes and gathering his thoughts, he listened to my explanation that I had stupidly forgotten to ask my friends to bring their passports with them as we were only going to Hatta for brunch. He smiled. 'It happens all the time' he said as he hastily wrote some words on a pad of paper, tore it off and told me to give it to the guard in the kiosk. This I did and we were on our way again. Mental note: Never leave home without passports or other identification.

My daughter and I rarely prepared our own food. There were half a dozen Michelin star restaurants within a ten minute walk of the apartment and an entire smorgasbord of bars, eateries and fast food establishments. Jumeirah Beach Road, known locally as JBR passed right in front of my apartment and was a sight to behold, especially on Fridays when it became a slow parade of the most exotic vehicles known to man.

Owners loved to show off their pink Rolls-Royces, or bright red Ferraris, but the biggest show-offs of all were the Dubai Police who actually had a department called 'Dubai Police Classic Vehicles'. Their cars, painted in the standard Dubai police colours of cream with an olive stripe, included Bugattis, Lamborghinis, Maseratis and just about every other expensive brand of car imaginable. The immaculately dressed officers would park up on the road to allow tourists to take pictures of them posing in front of their cars. It was of course a PR stunt, but a very effective one.

The key word in Dubai was excess. Everything had to be the biggest, highest, longest, or fastest. It was the keynote of its success. Having basically run out of its limited quantities of oil back in the eighties it was forced to re-invent itself from a quiet backwater into an international destination for tourism and business. The Dubai International Finance Centre (DIFC) was a half a square mile of business in the heart of Dubai where business was conducted, not in accordance with local laws, but in accordance with the laws of England.

If Sheikh Mohammed wished anything to be done then it was done. There was no opposition, indeed Sheikh Mohammed was a very popular leader and he certainly knew how to look after his people. Spurning chauffeur driven limousines, he frequently drove himself to events in his white Mercedes jeep with little or no security, confident in the love and respect of those around him. I doubt that many national leaders could afford to act in this way.

Chapter 36

Time to Leave

Towards the end of 2014, although the business situation was much the same, I just wasn't enjoying the job anymore. Due to the company's financial position, I worried about various aspects of the job and found myself unable to switch off outside of working hours. This was something which I had never experienced before. A number of other factors were also coming into play, my parents were becoming increasingly frail and I had just turned sixty two. As much as I enjoyed many aspects of life in Dubai, I no longer needed it. I felt that it was time for me to hang up my boots and return home.

I decided to go and see the chairman and let him know of my decision. He clearly didn't want me to leave, but understood my reasons. He asked me not to tell anyone else for the time being and requested that I stay on until they could appoint a successor, which I was happy to do. My final day of work would be January 31st, 2015.

Surrendering my Emirates residency was a time-consuming process, everything being checked to ensure that I had no outstanding debts etc. I was somewhat surprised one day when my government affairs manager came into my office and informed me that he would have to clear a number of speeding convictions before he could proceed any further. 'How many are there?' I asked.

'Well,' he said, 'there are five outstanding which need to be paid.'

'It sounds as though there have been more,' I replied.

'Oh yes,' he replied, 'many more, but I didn't want to bother you with them before and have been paying them from the company accounts for the past year.' Goodness me! I thought that I had been lucky to avoid the speed cameras, but in fact I hadn't. I thanked him for taking care of me, but asked him to let me know how many fines he had paid and instructed him to deduct the amounts from my final settlement. I'm a little embarrassed to confess that I had over thirty speeding fines during my eighteen months in the Emirates, though they were only fines. I obviously had not been going 'too fast'!

And so I bid farewell to the desert on January 31st 2015. My daughter would remain in Dubai for the present time and I managed to arrange another apartment for her to share with some friends. I knew that I would miss the place, but I wasn't sorry to leave, I had completed twenty-five years in that part of the world and it had changed my life in so many ways. From the young twenty-six year old who got off a plane in Saudi Arabia on that hot summer evening in 1979, thinking that it would only be for a couple of years, to the sixty-two-year-old man about to retire.

Where had the time gone?

Chapter 37

The Last Grain of Sand

Just when you think you have shaken the last grain of sand out of your shoes, something happens to remind you that in many ways you never really leave Arabia.

So it was that some eighteen months after my retirement and departure from Dubai, my wife and I set off on a holiday to India. We would fly to New Delhi on Emirates Airlines via Dubai where there would be a four hour wait for the connecting flight. We passed the time by reading and perusing the extensive duty free shops in the terminal. At last the flight was called and we made our way to the gate. Producing our passports and boarding passes, we handed them to one of the Emirates staff. He looked at my passport and then handed it to two other men wearing dark suits, who had suddenly appeared.

They studied my passport and were comparing it with a sheet of paper with Arabic script and worryingly, with what appeared to be my photograph at the top. They asked me my name and said, 'You are not allowed to board, you must come with us.'

'What's this all about?' I asked.

'There is a case to answer,' was their only reply. My wife apparently was free to board the flight, it was only me that they were interested in. 'Go, go' they said to her, but quite naturally my wife was going to do nothing of the sort.

'Our suitcases have already been loaded onto the plane' I insisted. They replied that they had not in fact been loaded and were still here in the airport.

It was clear that I was going nowhere. Thoughts were running frantically through my mind. What case? When I had departed the UAE some eighteen months earlier my residency had been cancelled correctly and I had no outstanding debts, fines or 'cases' of any nature. We were led out of the transit area and through a maze of stairwells and corridors to the airport police station. My passport was once again checked by the policeman on duty and, satisfied that it matched the details on the mysterious piece of paper, the two plain clothed men departed. The policeman indicated that we should take a seat.

I racked my brain to think what this might all be about, but couldn't for the life of me come up with any plausible explanation. After ten minutes, the policeman summoned me to the desk and advised me that a company in Abu Dhabi had taken out a case personally against me for an unpaid debt. It was a car rental company. At last it became clear, this was not a personal debt at all. At some point at least eighteen months ago, I had signed on behalf of the company, a contract for the supply of some vehicles and six months after my retirement, a dispute must have arisen over the amount of money actually owed.

The concept of limited liability does not exist throughout much of Arabia and, in accordance with UAE law, in the event of any dispute, the company was entitled to take out a case, not only against the company whom I represented at that time, but also against the person who had signed the contract. Me!

I was fingerprinted, had a retinal image scan and was then

taken, along with my wife, to a larger station which I assumed, was the main police station at the airport. We were told to take a seat in a waiting area containing two rows of plastic seats facing the main desk. A hall led off from one end of the main counter containing a row of three solid doors with a tiny window in each.

Periodically, a policemen would walk down, open a small sliding panel over the window and peer inside. They were obviously cells. I continued to sit in the waiting area with my wife, wondering how I could find a way out of this. I had more questions than answers. How much money was involved? Was my former employer still in existence? How long would I be detained? If I was going to be locked up, where would my wife go?

One of my chief concerns was that if I was going to be held, my phone would be taken from me and I would no longer be able to contact my wife. If she checked into a hotel somewhere, I wouldn't know where, or how I would be able to get in touch with her. My daughter and most of my acquaintances had left Dubai and I didn't have the contact details with me of any that might still be there.

I rustled through my wallet and found one of my old business cards and made a hasty phone call to my former company. To my great relief, the call was answered and I asked to speak to the government affairs man who amazingly turned out to be Sami, who had worked for me during the time I was there.

Once he had got over the shock of hearing my voice after such a long time, I told him that I was presently sitting in a police station in Dubai and didn't know how, or when I would get out. He asked me to put him on to one of the policemen and they had a brief conversation in Arabic after which, the policeman handed the phone back to me.

Sami informed me that he hadn't been aware that anyone had taken out a case against me, but would find out and deal with the matter as quickly as he could. The problem was that it was Thursday evening, the day before the weekend and nothing was likely to happen before the following Saturday, or more likely Sunday, the first working day of the following week.

At least someone was now aware of my predicament and might be able to assist, but what I needed right now, was to sort out some accommodation for my wife. She had a sudden flash of inspiration. One of her cousins had a brother-in-law who was working in Dubai and so she rang her cousin in the UK, obtained her brother-in-law's contact details and managed to speak to him explaining the situation. His name was Charles and he proved to be an absolute star. He told her that he would come down to the airport police station right away and do whatever was necessary.

This was good news, but before he arrived, the police who were evidently growing impatient with the fact that I had remained seated in the waiting area after being formally identified and fingerprinted, decided that it was time for me to be locked up. I told my wife to remain in the waiting area until Charles arrived while I was led down the corridor to the cells, fortunately with my mobile phone still with me.

The cell measured ten feet by six feet. Wooden benches ran the length of each wall and the floor was tiled. There was no window save for the little glass opening in the door, covered by a sliding panel which could only be opened from the outside. A single fluorescent strip light provided illumination.

At least there weren't any bars! I sat down on the bench and put my head in my hands, wondering how the hell I had ended up here. I glanced at my watch, it was nine in the evening. We should have been in India by now and starting a wonderful holiday.

After half an hour, I heard raised voices outside and the door opened. In walked an Englishman who introduced himself as Charles. Thank goodness! He assured me that my wife would be all right and he would take her back to the villa which he shared with his wife and their son. He also told me that I would probably not be released for the time being until the matter was resolved. We exchanged mobile phone numbers and he left. As bad as this was, at least I knew that my wife was in good hands and that my former company government affairs representative was working on the case. That at least, is what I hoped.

I sat on the bench leaning my back against the wall with my eyes closed. I knew that sleep would be impossible. I soon realised that I had not eaten, or had a drink for more than six hours. I banged on the door a number of times before a policeman came. I told him that I needed water and to use the bathroom. He led me through the now deserted police station waiting room to a nearby public toilet. Fortunately there was a drinking fountain inside. The policeman waited outside until I had finished before escorting me back to the cell. It looked like I was going to be locked up here, at least for the night.

I resumed my position on the bench and rested my head against the wall. I closed my eyes with a million thoughts and scenarios running through my head. Half an hour later, I heard the jangle of keys in the door. A policeman ushered in a middle aged man who looked about ten years younger than me. We introduced ourselves and it turned out that he was American who had also been in transit, en route from New York to Hong Kong and that he too had been apprehended as he tried to board his connecting flight.

We swapped stories about our time in the Middle East and he told me that he'd been involved in a business deal with one of the local princes which had ended badly. From the situation he described, I took some comfort in the thought that his predicament sounded a hell of a lot worse than mine.

We talked for an hour or so and then tried to get some sleep. He lay on the floor and I resumed my posture on the bench, head resting against the wall, but found sleep impossible. An hour later, the cell door opened and three oriental men were ushered in. I could tell that they were Filipinos and that they appeared really scared. They didn't seem to want to enter into any conversations and spent the next few hours whispering quietly to each other in Tagalog. Over the next few hours in the windowless room, I checked my watch constantly.

At four thirty in the morning, the door was opened by two different policemen. They entered the cell and read out four names from a sheet of paper, my name and those of the three Filipinos. The noise awoke the American and I told him that I was being taken somewhere else. We wished each other the best of luck and he turned over and went back to sleep. The policemen produced handcuffs which they placed around our wrists with our hands in front of us. I had been in a few scrapes in my time, but never imagined in my wildest dreams, that I would ever find myself in handcuffs.

We were clearly being moved, but to where? Bizarrely, my main concern at that moment was the fact that we would undoubtedly be taken out through the airport concourse and

I was worried that I might be seen in handcuffs by someone I knew. I managed to pull down the sleeves of my fleece to hide the shiny 'bracelets' and followed the policemen outside the terminal. Fortunately there were very few people around at that hour.

The three Filipinos and I were put into a windowless van parked at the kerbside and we were driven off to who knew where. One of the Filipinos asked one of the policemen where we were headed, but received only the answer that we were being taken from a five star cell to a one star cell. I suppose he thought that was funny.

After a twenty minute drive, the van pulled to a stop and I was asked to get out, while the three Filipinos were instructed to remain inside. Once outside the van, my handcuffs were removed and, looking up in the semi-darkness, saw the familiar and unmistakeable sight of the high-rise buildings at the northern end of Sheikh Zayed Road. I was in the middle of the city and thankfully hadn't been taken to some god-forsaken prison out in the desert.

One of the policemen led me inside a large police station, showed me to a room and asked me to wait in one of the chairs. A few moments later another young policeman entered. He seemed pleasant enough, asking me where I was from and which football team I supported. He had someone bring me a cup of tea and explained to me in perfect English that a case had been brought against me in the Dubai courts by a company based in Abu Dhabi. Until the case was settled, they would continue to hold my passport and I would not be allowed to leave the country. I would however no longer remain in custody.

It seemed that I would have to arrange some kind of

agreement whereby the case against me could be withdrawn and my passport returned. I walked out of the police station into the cool, early morning air. I was free, but not free to leave the country. It was Friday and I knew that nothing would happen until the following day at the earliest. I called my wife and told her that I had been released.

Charles came to pick me up and once back at his villa, I was made very comfortable and I began to focus on what needed to be done to get out of my predicament. The senior management of my former company would now be aware of the situation, relayed to them as a result of my conversation with Sami. He had mentioned that the finance director with whom I had always had a good relationship, was still with the company. What I did not yet know was exactly how much the car rental company claimed they were owed. I would not be able to obtain this information until the following day at the earliest.

I had a restless night, my mind once again running through all the various scenarios. Perhaps the amount of money was extremely large, perhaps my former employer was still in financial difficulties. Perhaps I would have to pay the plaintiff company in order to get my passport back. It might turn out to be a very expensive passport.

It was beginning to concern me that if one company succeeded in obtaining money owed to them by bringing a case against me personally, then others might do the same while I was in the UAE. Saturday morning arrived and I got straight on the phone to the finance director who, worryingly was not picking up my calls. I called Sami who told me they were going to speak to the car rental company, later that day.

The following day, I called again and managed to get through to the finance director. He assured me that they were sorting it out and that there was no need to worry. I suspected that in true Arabian style, they were negotiating to agree a price somewhat lower than the value of the claim against me. I didn't care how much they paid as long as I got my passport back. I was still nervous about word on the street, well aware that people talk and if one company could get payment by taking out a case against me, then others could do so as well.

Another day passed and still no word. I made repeated calls to the office, but no-one seemed to be available and despite leaving many messages, no-one returned my calls. I had perhaps naively thought that this might be resolved within a couple of days and that I could be on my way, but things never run that smoothly in that part of the world. I decided that I would try to hurry things along, so on Tuesday, I rented a car and drove down to the office in Abu Dhabi. I would sit in my old office until the matter was settled.

It seemed strange retracing my old daily commute down the highway from Dubai to Abu Dhabi after eighteen months. The office looked just the same and there were many familiar faces to be seen from my time there. I introduced myself to my replacement and we had a cup of tea and chatted about how the company was doing. Despite a chronic shortage of liquidity it had managed to complete some of the projects which had started during my tenure, though he declined to say whether they had actually made any money.

At last the finance director and government affairs man showed up. It had all been agreed they said and the company representative of the car rental company would go with myself and Sami to the Dubai police headquarters and meet with the captain of police. For some reason however, this meeting could not take place until Thursday morning at nine.

I woke bright and early and got a taxi to the police station from where I had been released a week earlier. I was fifteen minutes early, but typically no-one else was there. There was no-one there at nine and still no-one there at nine thirty. At last, and to my great relief, Sami and another man showed up at ten. This was bang on time for most Arabs. We went into the captain's office and I was pleased to see that he had my passport on his desk. He asked Sami and the other man whether the matter had now been settled which they confirmed and then asked the plaintiff's representative whether he was formally dropping the case against me, to which he assented.

Signatures and company stamps were then affixed to a number of documents and the captain handed me my passport for which I had to sign. That was it, I was free to go. It had been a week to the day since I had first been apprehended at the airport. It seemed like a month.

I remained concerned that another company might seek to emulate this method of extracting payment. I therefore headed straight for the nearest Emirates Airlines office and booked one-way tickets home for my wife and I, that evening.

I have never been a nervous flyer, but I breathed a sigh of relief once the plane had left the runway. The bright, twinkling lights of Dubai gradually faded into the distance as I said my last farewell to this strange though now familiar land.

A land which would forever be entwined with my own personal history.

THE END

Afterword

I have an old framed map in my study, created by the seventeenth century cartographer, Herman Moll. It is a map of the Arabian Peninsula and was given to me as a farewell gift by my former colleagues.

The lower part of the peninsula bears the legend; 'Happy Arabia', an anglicised reference to the land known to the Romans as Arabia Felix. The map may not be geographically, or historically accurate, but it eloquently sums up the feelings I have for that part of the world.

Retired for five years at the time of writing, my memories of Arabia remain as clear as ever and they are predominantly happy ones. The stories contained in this book could not have happened without the support of my family and all the friends and colleagues, past and present from Arabia and all around the world, with whom I was fortunate enough to share these experiences.

I would like to thank them all for enriching my life in so many ways.